info@kinfolk.com
www.kinfolk.com

Kinfolk Magazine
328 NE Failing Street
Portland, Oregon 97212
Telephone: 503 946 8400
www.kinfolk.com

Printed in the United States of America

———————————————————

Publication Design by Amanda Jane Jones
Cover Photograph by Parker Fitzgerald

KINFOLK

SUBSCRIBE

VISIT WWW.KINFOLK.COM/SUBSCRIBE

FOUR VOLUMES EACH YEAR

_____

CONTACT US

If you have any questions or comments,
email us at *info@kinfolk.com*

SUBSCRIPTIONS

For questions regarding your subscription,
email us at *subscribe@kinfolk.com*

STOCKISTS

If you would like to carry *Kinfolk*,
email us at *distribution@kinfolk.com*

SUBMISSIONS

Send all submissions to
submissions@kinfolk.com

WWW.KINFOLK.COM

WELCOME

This issue is an ode to a country and culture we deeply admire. We cast a wide net and narrowed our focus on Japan, whose culture seems to echo many of the same principles we try to live by. We have learned a lot from what our writers, photographers and illustrators have contributed to this issue: There are mouthwatering recipes for all sorts of Japanese delectables. There are stunning photographs that put some lesser-known vistas under the spotlight. There are interviews with inspirational figures, and there are glimpses into the backstories of terms, traditions and practices. We don't consider ourselves cultural experts—our approach has been smaller in scope and more intimate and personal. This issue is a glimpse of Japan through the *Kinfolk* lens; it highlights what we love about this unique country, including the basic values (*mono no aware*, page 74; *wabi-sabi*, page 88), skills (indigo, page 66) and recipes (Wakame Cucumber Salad, page 100; Salt-Pickled Napa Cabbage, page 130) that come together to form the beautifully simple lifestyle we know is worth exploring.

We've taken our harvesting series to a farm on the mountain of the Izu Peninsula where cold, pristine water comes together with just the right balance of minerals for growing and gathering wasabi (page 36), that mysterious green paste we've enjoyed with sushi for years. We also visit a green tea plantation in Shizuoka (page 104), and venture out by boat with fishermen on an island in the Aichi Prefecture in southern Japan. It's doubtful that any one person, team or country can take credit for creating a simple, balanced, grounded food lifestyle, but many of our Japanese friends are excellent contenders. With that in mind, we are eager to share all the inspiration, recipes and tips we have learned from them.

You may notice that our subtitle changed from "A Guide for Small Gatherings" to "Discovering New Things to Cook, Make and Do." We can assure you that we won't stop coming up with ideas for small gatherings, but wanted to make *Kinfolk* more open in its coverage of home cooks, artists and makers, while remembering to keep things practical and approachable. We have also listened to your feedback and have been coming up with ideas to make a more readable magazine that matches our visual aesthetic.

NATHAN WILLIAMS, EDITOR OF KINFOLK MAGAZINE

NATHAN WILLIAMS
Editor
Portland, Oregon

KATIE SEARLE-WILLIAMS
Web Editor
Portland, Oregon

GAIL O'HARA
Copy Chief
Portland, Oregon

AMANDA JANE JONES
Senior Designer
Ann Arbor, Michigan

ERICA MIDKIFF
Copy Editor
Birmingham, Alabama

MARÍA DEL MAR SACASA
Recipe Editor
New York, New York

BEN BIONDO
Designer
Portland, Oregon

DOUG BISCHOFF
Distribution
Portland, Oregon

JOANNA HAN
Assistant Web Editor
Portland, Oregon

PAIGE BISCHOFF
Sales & Fulfillment
Portland, Oregon

PARKER FITZGERALD
Photographer
Portland, Oregon

ASIA RIKARD
Office Manager
Portland, Oregon

ANDREW & CARISSA GALLO
Filmmaker & Photographer
Portland, Oregon

SEAN DANAHER
Editorial Assistant
Portland, Oregon

DIANA YEN
Writer
Brooklyn, New York

ADRIANA JAIME
Editorial Assistant
Portland, Oregon

NICK BAINES
Writer
Bournemouth, United Kingdom

RILEY MESSINA
Florist & Writer
Portland, Oregon

JULIE POINTER
Gatherings & Community Engagement
Portland, Oregon

MICHELE BRINE
Order Fulfillment
Portland, Oregon

SAER RICHARDS
Writer
Brooklyn, New York

JAMES BOWDEN
Photographer
Bournemouth, United Kingdom

NIKAELA MARIE PETERS
Writer
Winnipeg, Canada

DANICA VAN DE VELDE
Writer
Perth, Australia

SETH SMOOT
Photographer
New York, New York

RICHARD ASLAN
Writer
Bristol, United Kingdom

TINA MINAMI DHINGRA
Translator
Tokyo, Japan

TAKAMASA KIKUCHI
Writer
London, United Kingdom

AYA MUTO
Writer
San Francisco, California

ERIN KUNKEL
Photographer
San Francisco, California

LOU MORA
Photographer
Los Angeles, California

LAURA DART
Photographer
Portland, Oregon

KATHRIN KOSCHITZKI
Photographer
Munich, Germany

JOSH LESKAR
Writer
San Francisco, California

ETHAN KAWASAKI
Writer
Sandy, Utah

REBECCA PARKER PAYNE
Writer
Richmond, Virginia

NANCY SINGLETON HACHISU
Writer
Kamikawa-machi, Japan

KENICHI EGUCHI
Writer
Tokyo, Japan

KATIE STRATTON
Painter
Dayton, Ohio

BRENT SEARLE
Writer
Shelley, Idaho

LISA MOIR
Stylist
San Francisco, California

HIDEAKI HAMADA
Photographer
Osaka, Japan

JOY KIM
Illustrator
Portland, Oregon

ALPHA SMOOT
Photographer
New York, New York

CHRIS & SARAH RHOADS
Photographers
Seattle, Washington

LOUISA THOMSEN BRITS
Writer
East Sussex, United Kingdom

ROMY ASH
Writer
Melbourne, Australia

KENDRA SMOOT
Stylist
Brooklyn, New York

SAWAKO AKUNE
Writer
Tokyo, Japan

GENTL & HYERS
Photographers
New York, New York

BOB STANLEY
Writer
London, United Kingdom

AUSTIN SAILSBURY
Writer
Copenhagen, Denmark

ASHLEY PAQUIN
Writer
Portland, Oregon

KELSEY B. SNELL
Proofreader
Washington, D.C.

KATIE RIDLEY
Illustrator
Atlanta, Georgia

JULIA GRASSI
Photographer
London, United Kingdom

SARAH BURWASH
Illustrator
Nova Scotia, Canada

ISAAC BESS
Writer
San Francisco, California

ASHLEY SCHLEEPER
Writer
Brooklyn, New York

MASAFUMI KAJITANI
Translator
Tokyo, Japan

MAYUMI NIIMI
Writer
New York, New York

ANAIS & DAX
Photographers
Los Angeles, California

HITOMI THOMPSON
Writer
Portland, Oregon

HIROYUKI SEO
Photographer
Los Angeles, California

RACHEL JONES
Writer
Brooklyn, New York

ADAM PATRICK JONES
Photographer
Brooklyn, New York

FEW

ONE

ENTERTAINING FOR ONE

一人の楽しみ方

○

LOVES FOOD, WILL TRAVEL

INTERVIEW BY TAKAMASA KIKUCHI & PHOTOGRAPHS BY JULIA GRASSI

For Eatrip's multimedia food director Yuri Nomura, life is one long eating trip. We dug deep to find out about her culinary background, food philosophy and her ideas about the way we eat now.

Through a garden off the street in a hidden corner of Tokyo, you'll find Eatrip, a restaurant run by food director Yuri Nomura, whose 10-year journey has involved a film, a magazine, a restaurant, catering, exhibitions, public relations and teaching. Her passion for conveying the joy of food is not limited by forms of expression. Here we find out all that she has learned about food and life.

WHAT WERE THE KEY MOMENTS THAT SHAPED WHO YOU ARE NOW?

My mother is a cookery teacher. I grew up in an environment surrounded by food. She loves to cook and invite people over for dinner. When I was a child, my home was often full of food, visitors and their laughter. I was especially impressed by how she welcomed visitors. Her welcoming manner has influenced who I am now.

HOW DID YOU START YOUR CAREER IN THE FOOD INDUSTRY?

When I lived in London, I was studying cooking and became aware of Terence Conran. He was and is an influential designer and a pioneer of lifestyle design in Europe. He helped people realize that good design of space and everyday items relating to food such as tables, chairs, dishes, bowls, glasses and cutlery can enrich our lifestyle. Soon after coming back to Tokyo, I was offered a job as a chef at Idée Café, run by Japanese furniture company Idée. The restaurant was influenced by Conran's concepts, and my experience in London contributed to its progress.

YOU HAVE OFTEN WORKED WITH CREATIVE PEOPLE FROM DIFFERENT FIELDS. WHERE DID THE INSPIRATION FOR THIS COME FROM?

While working at Idée Café, I was involved in many catering events for creative companies. Clients often gave me free rein to arrange the whole event: decorating the space, choosing the tableware, the music and the food. I collaborated with designers and musicians on these events. For instance, I commissioned my favorite graphic designer to illustrate dishes according to an event's theme. These experiences inspired me to explore food through artistic expression.

WHAT MOTIVATED YOU TO MAKE THE FILM *EATRIP*?

At that time, LOHAS (Lifestyles of Health and Sustainability) was a very fashionable term in Japan. Although the fact that many people were conscious about organic food and sustainable ecology was good, the movement became rather superficial—it became just part of food marketing strategies. This made me want to express my ideas about the pleasure of life and food. I thought that film was the best medium to make my ideas about food accessible to people.

HOW HAVE YOUR CIRCUMSTANCES CHANGED AFTER COMPLETING THE FILM?

There has been a tremendous reaction from the audience, which I did not expect at all. I immediately understood that I was in a position to influence people potentially in a good or bad way. I started feeling more responsible about my actions, which deeply burdened me. When I was thinking of how I wished to engage with food and what I believed in, Alice Waters from Chez Panisse struck me as someone I respect for her influence as a female chef and her contribution to American society. I decided to work there to learn more about her food philosophy.

HOW WAS YOUR EXPERIENCE AT CHEZ PANISSE? DID YOU FIND WHAT YOU NOW BELIEVE IN?

I had a great time there and was working with very interesting chefs. We got along well and shared our philosophy of food. They hold an event called Open Restaurant in an art space, which is a food experiment in a cultural and social context. I invited them to Japan and we held Open Harvest together, which was very successful. A collective of Japanese chefs participated in it, and it totally changed their way of thinking about food. In fact, it was a life-changing experience for them. We then started Nomadic Kitchen together.

WHAT DOES NOMADIC KITCHEN DO?

Nomadic Kitchen visits a place and explores its regional nature and culture. We meet farmers and try to understand their production methods, and we also cook and hold gatherings with local people. Eatrip had an exhibition in Fukuoka, Kyushu Island, a few months ago. Nomadic Kitchen had a temporary kitchen in an art gallery and served food to guests on the last day of the exhibition. We visited local farmers and bought products directly from them. The Japanese are very nervous about food safety after the Fukushima nuclear disaster. In order for them to enjoy food without any fear or doubt, it is very important that they get transparent information about where a product has come from, who the farmer is or how it is made. A good relationship between a farmer, a chef and the consumer is based on trust and respect. That is how we should appreciate food.

WHAT IS YOUR FAVORITE FOOD?

I am interested in preserved food. It is a type of food made all over the world, yet each country has a different way of preservation depending on the culture, climate and nature. I make my own Japanese preserved food by adapting foreign preservation methods. For example, I make anchovy preserves with Japanese fish. The way in which you can preserve local products inspires me.

WHAT ARE YOU INTERESTED IN DOING NEXT?

I am learning the art of the Japanese tea ceremony. A guest is invited for a cup of tea with the host's thoughtful cares. A host intentionally decorates the tearoom with flowers and paintings and specially selects cups and sweets for the tea ceremony that are influenced by the guest's background or the season or climate. All the elements in the tea ceremony present a welcoming gesture. Being welcomed in such a way would enhance any guest's experience. ○

SUMMER HANDBOOK

WORDS BY ROMY ASH & ILLUSTRATIONS BY SARAH BURWASH

Things are heating up—yes, summer is here. While temperatures rise and the flip-flops come out, read our suggestions for making the best of this sultry season.

PRESERVING THE BOUNTY The limbs of trees sag heavy with fruit. Brambles, which tear at my clothes the rest of the year, are now bejeweled with berries. It's worth any scratch to reach past the thorns to pick a berry that is bursting with sweetness. All the plants and trees are going wild, and there is so often an overabundance of fruit. Preserving this bounty is hard, hot work, but it is rewarding. When the days turn dark and short, there'll be jars of summer fruits, jams, pickles and chutneys, still tasting of sunshine. And in the meantime, there's a pantry full of shining jars to simply be admired or gifted to friends.

A DEEP SWIM Way out past the breakers, or in the deep of a lake, I like to just float. With ears underwater, I listen to the sound of silence and watch the clouds overhead. Being in any large body of water is a powerful feeling, reminiscent of the womb. It's a great comfort. Yet being out of your depth can be terrifying; it requires a sense of surrender. A swim like this can shift your perspective and make any worry seem small.

ROAD TRIPS Leave the windows open, have a summer mixtape ready, pack cold water and lemonade and follow that black lick of a road out of town. Travel with a friend and notice that intimacies are shared easily when there's nothing to do but watch the landscape blur.

A SOLO HIKE The rhythm of walking is a kind of meditation. Paradoxically, the movement brings stillness. With no one to talk to, there is time to notice the eagle catching an updraft overhead, as well as the tiny wrens hopping from branch to branch in the undergrowth. In this contemplative state everything is heightened. As the day draws on, with physical exhaustion comes happiness.

THE COOL CHANGE Where I live, the weather pattern shifts dramatically from one moment to the next. A sweltering day can be turned on its head with the cool change, a wind that blows from the Antarctic, as if straight across the ice. It's a cold wind that surges through the house, slamming doors and blowing papers. It's a wind that reminds me to cherish the heat when I may have been cursing it. It reminds me that everything is always changing—to live in that sweltering moment, to hurry up and get to the pool before the cool change blows in.

BEACHCOMBING A friend and I recently combed a beach for food-shaped rocks. By the end of the day, we had assembled a feast. Five burgers, with pale round rocks for the buns and dark flat rocks for the patties. A steak and chips, sausages. Not a healthy meal, but that was what the ocean gave us. A tide can change the shape of the beach. Each high tide washes away the day and begins again. It brings a new set of treasures: a seaweed necklace, shells, a shark's egg, flotsam and jetsam or more hamburger rocks. It's such a surprise and joy to see what the ocean has gifted each day anew.

EATING ONLY COOL THINGS I am loath to turn the oven on. The house itself is hot enough to cook in. What's needed is cooling meals, with no fuss, that only need to be thrown together and dressed. I like to slice big heirloom tomatoes, picked straight from the garden, and serve them with only a pinch of sea salt. Or I make a salad of garden greens, hard-boiled eggs and white anchovies. If anything is to be cooked, it must be barbecued. For dessert, mango is blitzed, stirred with coconut milk and frozen into icy poles. I eat dinner outside, and only once the sun has set.

SEARCHING FOR THE SHADE In winter, when working in the city, the challenge is to find the strips of sunlight between the shade of tall buildings, a moment when the city opens up and throws a bit of sky and sunshine. But in summer, a shift happens. I find myself searching instead for the shade, hanging in the lee side of buildings. On the weekends I want to head to the hills, to somewhere ferny and mossy. Somewhere a waterfall gouges a pool, where the water is its deepest green, where river pebbles are smooth under my feet and the water is cold enough to make a new skin.

A FAMILY HOLIDAY HOUSE Unchanged from the '60s, my friend's beach house is filled with furniture her grandfather made. The crockery is all pale peach, dusty green and Made in England. The windows and doors open wide onto the veranda, and there's a view to the curve of the beach and the hills that roll up from it. The mark of the grandparents is everywhere, but now, it's just the grandkids and their friends who visit, arriving late on a Friday night from the city, waking early to walk the cliff path down to the sea. These houses are redolent with childhood nostalgia. The floorboards are worn, soft as memory. ○

THE LANDSCAPE OF FLAWS

WORDS BY DANICA VAN DE VELDE & PHOTOGRAPHS BY LAURA DART

*While many aspects of Japanese culture are marked by restraint,
order and perfection, gardens are informed by* wabi-sabi. *Our writer fell
in love with these bucolic wonderlands after seeing them in a film.*

I fell in love with the aesthetics of Japanese gardening not through visiting Japan, but via the cinematic imagery in Sofia Coppola's *Lost in Translation* (2003). Specifically, it was a vignette set in the Zen gardens in Kyoto that piqued my interest in the Japanese approach. After following Scarlett Johansson's character on a solitary train journey to Kyoto, we watch her quietly wander through the temples and pagodas of the gardens. Like the best filmmakers, Coppola and cinematographer Lance Acord take the viewer on a journey by way of the images of stepping-stones in the water lily ponds and the ancient trees adorned with handmade paper blooms. As someone who had never visited Japan, I was entranced by this dreamlike vista. There was something about Kyoto's beautifully stark wintery landscape that mirrored the incompleteness of, and the loneliness interwoven into, the human relationships in the film; the gardens revealed their own narrative of desire and loss.

On reflection, I realized that my interest in Japanese methods of tending to flora was sparked much earlier, during my teenage years, when my mother began taking *ikebana* classes. For the duration of her night course, she would return every Tuesday evening with a floral arrangement grander and more avant-garde than the last. I'd never particularly cared for traditional flower arranging, but I immediately connected with the minimalist and disciplined nature of ikebana, in which the composition of flowers and foliage is less evocative of garden beds than of architectural structures. My mother's foray into cultivating a small collection of bonsai, neatly displayed on our kitchen windowsill, extended my fascination with what I perceived to be a strangely ornamental form of simplicity.

Although there are a wide variety of styles within the broader genre of Japanese gardens, it is the attentiveness to asymmetry and natural harmony that has always captured my attention. The Japanese word *shakkei*, which means "borrowed scenery," best encapsulates the concept behind Japanese gardening, which is inspired by the wild landscape. In distilling the natural order of the surrounding environment into both public and private gardens, Japanese designers and horticulturalists offer a very different view than the one I was exposed to growing up in suburban Australia. Where the gardens on my street were created in competition with the natural landscape, Japanese gardens emphasize the beauty in the everyday, railing against excess and producing visual themes that are grandiose in their modesty.

"Although there are a wide variety of styles within the broader genre of Japanese gardens, it is the attentiveness to asymmetry and natural harmony that has always captured my attention"

In contrast to the rose bushes, cut grass and potted pansies featured in the gardens of my youth, Japanese gardens are composed of a number of elements, including rocks, sand and pebbles; water features in the form of ponds, cascades and streams; architectural accents such as pavilions, lanterns and bridges; and humble displays of greenery and flowers. Although many aspects of Japanese culture are defined by restraint, orderliness and perfection, gardens do not necessarily follow a strictly manicured schema. Rather, the layout and organization are informed by the principles of the ancient Japanese philosophy of *wabi-sabi*.

While a number of writers and cultural scholars have given various definitions of this concept, "wabi" is generally aligned with the melancholic ache of romantic longing and "sabi" with the unfolding of time. Placing these two words together evokes an aesthetic of seclusion, imperfection and frugality that sheds light on the visual appeal of objects and landscapes that are blemished, perishing, fleeting and uncultivated. Bearing this description in mind, the fact that I had an overwhelmingly emotional response to the gardens in *Lost in Translation* probably had less to do with filmic manipulation than with the symbolism of the topography captured on film.

The celebration of inconsistencies and weathering that I find particularly appealing in Japanese gardens is articulated in the focus on miniaturization in both large-scale gardens and the aesthetics of bonsai planting. Although I did not realize it as a young girl gazing at my mother's bonsai, the shaping techniques involved in trimming, pruning and wiring to achieve the twisted and coiled look of bonsai also reflect the concept of wabi-sabi. In representing the natural landscape on a smaller scale, bonsai rely on similar ideas of asymmetry and imperfection in an attempt to leave no trace of the intervention of the human hand. The simplicity of this ethos is something that I find both noble and touching; the absence of physical touch bespeaks an investment in nature to create spaces of contemplation, stillness and reverie.

For me, the appeal of Japanese gardening is ultimately found in this admirable conviction of redefining aesthetic attractiveness. In such environments, one is invited to assess what he or she perceives as visually appealing and to find beauty and grace in the rustic, unrefined and unassuming. ○

Danica van de Velde is a writer based in Perth, Western Australia.

INSTANT EXTRACTION

WORDS BY KENICHI EGUCHI & PHOTOGRAPHS BY LOU MORA

Spotlight on five of our favorite coffee shops across Tokyo.

LITTLE NAP / Little Nap is no ordinary café. Its size defines it as a coffee stand. Overlooking the back of Yoyogi Park, the café is in a residential neighborhood inhabited by Tokyo's creative population. Offering minimal seating, Little Nap represents the trend of Tokyo coffee stands—a reaction to the expensive rent. It embodies owner Daisuke Hamada's idea of how coffee should be enjoyed. Its contemporary laid-back design was inspired by the idea of a boot repairman's workshop. While he is equipped with the tools to brew coffee by hand, Hamada is also an expert at using both coffee and espresso machines. He can fine-tune the machines to fit the day's conditions, and there are few baristas with this expertise. But Hamada has his hands on everything. At the time we made our visit, he was busy designing a recording studio. He organizes music events and produces other coffee shops. He is the man behind Bridge in the downtown Kappabashi district, which is known for kitchen tools. He has an extension at Vacant in Harajuku. Bands frequent his shop when they're in town. People chat him up for information on what's going on in town, and you can tell he enjoys the company.

ADDRESS: 5-65-4 Yoyogi, Shibuya-ku / TELEPHONE: 03-3466-0074
9 a.m.–7 p.m. (Closed Mondays) / littlenap.jp

OMOTESANDO KOFFEE / K is for "koffee," "kiosk" and Kunitomo. Eiichi Kunitomo is no newcomer to the coffee business. In fact, he is considered a veteran of managing and producing coffee shops, which makes his move to open Omotesandō Koffee even more interesting. The kiosk is nestled in a traditional Japanese house, off a side street in Omotesandō. Through the wooden gate, you step over the porch where previous residents may have left their shoes. Now taking center stage is a square counter with a Cimbali machine where Kunitomo and his staff serve coffee to order. Despite the trend in drip, he works with machines, and the cappuccino and macchiato—in a choice of glass, ceramic or paper cups—can be sipped in the small garden or taken out. There is no seating indoors, which was Kunitomo's way to cope with the high rent and still serve quality coffee. He is polite and meticulous, wearing a pharmacist-style coat with a cube logo on the front, and there are cube motifs everywhere; even the cakes are in small cubes. The small cube container made of used coffee grounds makes a good souvenir, but they go fast, so grab one while you can.

ADDRESS: 4-15-3 Jingumae, Shibuya-ku / TELEPHONE: 03-5413-9422
10 a.m.–7 p.m. (may close without notice) / ooo-koffee.com

BREAD, ESPRESSO & / During your stroll through Omotesandō, you may encounter people with paper bags that say Bread, Espresso &. These are from a café and bakery run by Kunitomo of Omotesandō Koffee, which is close enough if you need to nibble on something or want to sit down—past the *tonkatsu* restaurant Maisen and the Lotus Café. Once you're there, you'll smell the freshly baked pastries that are coming straight out of the oven. Some of the loaves come in small cubes. In the warmer months, it would be nice to sit outside. The coffee is probably superior at Omotesandō Koffee, but at Bread, Espresso &, they will still brew coffee to order. Another establishment that Kunitomo is involved with is Kitsuné, which he runs with his friends Gildas and Masaya, near the Omotesandō crossing; if you visit, you can see the variety of work he does.

ADDRESS: 3-4-9 Jingumae, Shibuya-ku / TELEPHONE: 03-5410-2040
8 a.m.–8 p.m. / bread-espresso.jp

BE A GOOD NEIGHBOR / Probably the smallest of the bunch, Be a Good Neighbor is definitely a coffee stand. Four or five people will easily pack the counter. The friendly manager behind the counter, Kajihara, is keen on introducing you to the various ways of enjoying coffee. When we were there, he let us sample extremely light Ethiopian beans using the AeroPress. From what looked like weak coffee came a rich floral aroma, and it was the perfect coffee on a day when we had had too many cups already. Be a Good Neighbor is in Landscape territory. Shinichiro Nakahara of Landscape Products, who is well connected with Heath Ceramics in California, opened the furniture store Playmountain near Sendagaya Elementary School. The area features some of his own ventures such as Tas Yard (a café serving food with a pop-up shop for local wares), Chigo for children's products, as well as Papier Labo (original paper products) and Tembea (a quality Japanese canvas bag brand). It's a great area to check out.

ADDRESS: 3-51-6 Sendagaya, Shibuya-ku / TELEPHONE: 03-5770-3195
Monday–Friday, 8:30 a.m.–6 p.m. / Saturday, Sunday and holidays, 11:30 a.m.–5 p.m.
beagoodneighbor.net/sendagaya

CAFÉ BACH / Many people used to say coffee in Tokyo was expensive. I used to think so too. But then, with all the franchise coffee shops around, you have to wonder if you're getting your money's worth. Café Bach is a coffee shop that has been around for 40 years, from when the area was called Sanya, almost a synonym for skid row. It's near a bridge called Namidabashi (tear bridge) that became a popular backdrop for a classic manga, and nowadays the flophouses cater to foreign travelers. Café Bach has explored the Japanese way of brewing coffee and has trained people who now run coffee shops all over Japan. They are students of the Bach school, and Mamoru Taguchi is their mentor. He holds what he calls "seminars" for free, for whoever's interested in delivering a decent drip. Sure, it is old-school, but somehow—now that contemporary coffee enthusiasts have seen the world and come back to their roots, and now that the trend is in drips—he is much respected. So it might be a good idea to include this in your list of destinations and book a seminar.

ADDRESS: 1-23-9 Nihonzutsumi, Taito-ku / TELEPHONE: 03-3879-2669
8:30 a.m.–9 p.m. (closed Fridays) / bach-kaffee.co.jp

Kenichi Eguchi is a writer, editor and book translator. He offers workshops and catering services under the name "food+things" and runs the online film magazine Outside in Tokyo. ○

渋い
SHIBUI

勿体無い
MOTTAINAI

WORDS TO LIVE BY

Toss out the self-help guides and use these time-tested concepts from Japan to create a better life and be a better soul.

WORDS BY HITOMI THOMPSON
ILLUSTRATIONS BY JOY KIM

01 渋い *Shibui*

Shibui describes a tangy bitterness. In food, it may be undesirable—a rawness in spring mountain vegetables that needs to be cooked out, or a flavor present in unripe persimmons. When people are described as "shibui," the image is of a silver-haired man in a tailored suit, with a hint of a bad-boy aura about him. It is a subdued edge, an acquired taste appreciated by adults.

02 勿体無い *Mottainai*

This is a phrase grandmas say a lot. Not just to encourage you to eat the remaining rice in your bowl (the teardrops of farmers), but to encourage you to be more outgoing and seize the day, because there is so much you have to offer the world and so much the world can also give you. This is a phrase to remind you not to waste things or opportunities.

生き甲斐

IKIGAI

故郷

FURUSATO

一期一会

ICHI-GO ICHI-E

---

03 生き甲斐 *Ikigai*

This is what you live for, the passion and the purpose of your life. Have you found your *ikigai* yet? It is the joy found in living, whether it is your job, volunteer work, your family or your friends. It is what you are trying to achieve from this life that you were given.

04 故郷 *Furusato*

Furusato means where you are from, your hometown and birthplace. It made you who you are today; it is where you go back to visit relatives and pay respects to your ancestors. You can have a second furusato, a place where your heart feels at home—you give to it like it gives to you.

05 一期一会 *Ichi-go Ichi-e*

This literally means "one life, one meeting/party/gathering/chance." It's a word from tea ceremony that reminds us to treasure each moment, because everything just happens once in life. This gathering will never happen in the same way again. ○

KING OF CLAY

Ceramicist Ryota Aoki isn't content to just be an amazing potter;
he also has a personal mission to help improve the pottery industry and
ensure a place in the canon for his own work.

INTERVIEW BY BRENT SEARLE & PHOTOGRAPHS BY HIROYUKI SEO
TRANSLATED BY TINA MINAMI DHINGRA

Pottery in Japan is as much a visual art as it is functional in purpose. And it's ancient—century upon century of experimenting has been done with earthen materials to shape products of beauty, purpose and decoration. Dynasties rose and fell, and pottery was at the center of disputes on more than one occasion.

From clay, porcelain and glazes come hot-fired teaware, rice bowls, jars, dishes, vases and ornamental creations. The eyes that envision and the hands that create these works of art are greatly honored in Japan. The culture is imbued with it.

A new set of eyes and hands that are shaping the future of pottery belong to Ryota Aoki, who blends historic and modern in his pottery. His works range from delicate and gentle soft, white porcelain dishes and teaware to Manganese vases and even Gothic-looking crowns and skulls. We chatted with him about his creative process, organizations, events and influences.

TELL US HOW YOU GOT STARTED IN POTTERY. WHAT INTERESTED YOU IN THIS TYPE OF WORK AND ART FORM?

When I was in college, I realized that a person's day is divided into three parts: eight hours of work, eight hours of sleep, eight hours of doing what you love. It was then when I thought, Why not do what you love for your work? After realizing this, I started to look for a job that I love.

First, I started to make clothes and accessories. I had tried working at so many different types of part-time jobs to find something that most resonated with me, but I hadn't had the "this is it" kind of feeling. But one day, I attended a pottery class. The moment I touched the soil for my first piece of work, it left such a powerful impression on me. That's when I decided I would be a potter.

What's amazing about pottery is that it can last for 3,000 years. Pottery dating back to B.C. still exists, even if it wasn't baked properly. Because my ambition is to become Japan's representative, I have a Japanese flag hanging in front of my potter's wheel. It would make me so happy to know that if someone 1,000 or 2,000 years later were to inquire about past Japanese artists, Ryota Aoki would be mentioned. I would like to leave my work for that reason.

POTTERY IS HIGHLY REVERED IN JAPAN AND OFTEN THE SKILLS AND TECHNIQUES ARE HANDED DOWN IN FAMILY TRADITIONS. HAS POTTERY BEEN IN YOUR FAMILY, OR ARE YOU THE FIRST?

There are no direct family members who do what I do—none of my relatives either. I would be the first generation. It's definitely true that skills and techniques from a potter are handed down in the house and are not shared. I first studied the basics, and then I moved on to researching the techniques and creating a glaze. Through this process, I'm confident that I can be the only one to create this kind of work and glaze as you can see in much of my work—like my wine glass.

WHO ARE SOME OF THE PEOPLE OR WHAT ARE SOME TIME PERIODS THAT INFLUENCE YOUR WORK? ARE YOU ATTEMPTING TO RE-CREATE THE PAST IN YOUR WORK, ENERGIZE THE FUTURE, OR BOTH?

The past: There is a traditional saying that has two meanings: One is to inherit (pass on) the "shape." Another is to inherit (pass on) the "spirit."

The most prosperous time in Japanese pottery history was from 400 years ago, during the Momoyama period [1573–1615]. This period's influence can be seen in today's work—modern potters have appropriated the Shino *chawan* (Shino tea bowl) and Oribe *chawan* (Oribe tea bowl) from this era. Although I do think this is important, the idea reminds me of karaoke. It's kind of like a singer who is trying really hard to re-create a song from the Beatles. Isn't that just a cover band? It's important to inherit the "spirit" of the past (instead of the "shape"). This means to learn and inherit the spirit, the kind of mind-set potters had in the past. Potters from 400 years ago must have had a feeling that left them wanting to create something new for the world. That's the kind of spirit I'd like to inherit and keep alive.

An English potter named Lucie Rie has influenced me the most. I love her work, but I also respect her for committing herself to researching and producing a new type of glaze. I've been influenced by her spirit and would like to carry that on for myself. Koie Ryoji, Kitaoji Rosanjin and countless other Japanese potters have also influenced me.

The future: By the time I was in my mid-20s, I was able to earn a living through my work. I was very content and at peace with becoming a professional potter. Since then I decided that I wanted to give back and pay respect to the art of pottery. I strongly believe that I could give back to this art form by being active in the ceramics industry. Currently, I am working toward the goal of creating more opportunities so that the next generation of potters is able to earn a living through the craft.

Every summer I am involved with an event called Ikeyan where many young potters and students gather around the theme of "how to make a living in ceramics." This is not traditionally a topic that is spoken about in schools, and every year, about 150 to 200 people participate. Each participant brings two cups they have made themselves: one to use to introduce themselves to the group—this is a great tool for people to connect based around their work—and another to use for critique and feedback. We gather 10 of the most relevant and famous gallery curators and ask them to choose the top 10 pieces to be eligible for a solo or group exhibition. My intention is to take part in creating the next generation of potters. I also want to address how potters can make a living all over the world. With this ambition, I recently announced a social network platform for ceramics called Potter.

YOUR POTTERY SPANS AN ECLECTIC MIX, FROM VERY ELEGANT PORCELAIN TABLEWARE TO DARKER MATERIALS IN VASES AND EVEN WHAT APPEARS TO BE CLAY AND METALS IN CROWNS AND SKULLS. WHAT INSPIRES YOUR WORK, AND HOW DO YOU CHOOSE YOUR MATERIALS?

I want to create something that's never been seen in the history of ceramics in Japan and worldwide. In order to achieve my goal, I produce and study up to 15,000 glazes a year. I make a decision based on the test piece. It's all very intuitive and I know when a certain glaze is *it*.

THIS MUST BE LONG WORK—AND HOT WORK AT TIMES BEING AROUND A KILN. HOW MANY HOURS DO YOU WORK EACH DAY? WHAT DO YOU LIKE TO DO WHEN YOU AREN'T WORKING?

Every day out of the year is like a holiday because I don't consider this to be work—I am doing what I love to do. My production time is from 9 a.m. to 9 p.m. I don't use a kiln with fire; mine is an electric kiln, so what I do is press a button—it's kind of like a big oven. I usually bake it for 16 hours.

When I am not producing work, I travel around the world to look at pottery. I meet different potters from around the world. Last year I was traveling one-third of the year. This year I gathered potters from all over the world at my studio in Gifu, Japan, to bring back knowledge to their home countries. This spring I hired staff members from Indonesia and Chile. I made sure to have everyone get a one-year visa so that they can take their time to take in the techniques and knowledge. ○

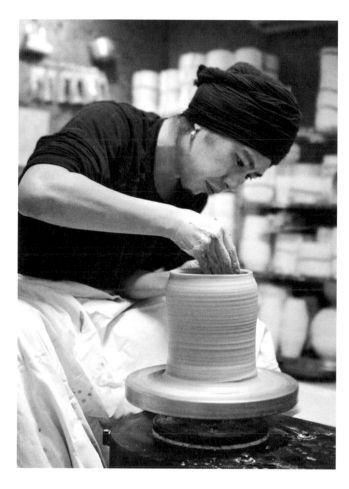

THE CUTTING EDGE

Treated carefully, a quality Japanese chef knife can be an extension of its owner and have a personality of its own. Here, a knife owner discusses the significance of managing the proper blade.

I received my first Japanese knife when I was 15, as a gift from my father when he took me on a trip to San Francisco. We went to a knife shop in Japantown where my dad got a *yanagi* and I got an *usuba*. As I became a more dedicated cook and eventually a chef, he passed his yanagi on to me, and while it is not the most versatile of knives, it is still a cherished piece in my collection. I have since purchased many more knives, but my favorite and the one I use nearly every day is a Western-style *gyutou* that I purchased in Japan. A knife has this strange ability to develop its own personality—you get to know your knife after hours and hours of use over many years. The way you sharpen it and the way the metal wears and oxidizes all contribute to the way it cuts and feels in your hand.

The knife is unequivocally the most important tool in the kitchen: It is an icon in the culinary arts. Cooks get them tattooed on their bodies. You don't touch another cook's knives. A knife is one of the only tools professional chefs and cooks bring with them to their jobs, and cooking almost always begins with cutting. Whether you are slicing through pieces of delicate buttery *hamachi* or making a mirepoix for a stock, the first step is to take food and break it down into more manageable sizes using a knife. They say your end product will only be as good as your first step. If your knife is of poor quality, it will only do a great disservice to the food and the final result. When a tomato is at the pinnacle of ripeness, fresh off the vine and still warm from the sun, a dull knife will do nothing but mash and bruise the flesh, whereas a surgically sharp blade will glide through, leaving you with juicy, glistening slices of vibrant red, green or yellow tomato.

There are few hand tools that are as visually striking as Japanese knives, from the rich marbled Damascus steel and beautiful straight lines to the warm wooden handles and natural horn or bone bolsters. Japanese knives are made using forging techniques deeply rooted in the same process that has been used to make samurai swords for centuries; no other knife will be as sharp or cut as precisely and cleanly as a well-maintained Japanese knife.

The Japanese are known for sparing no attention to detail, and this strict discipline is clearly evident in their cuisine. As this food culture has evolved, master knife craftsmen have developed a vast array of knives, many of them designed for just one specific task in the kitchen. This expansive menagerie of knives really shows the love and respect the Japanese have for their food, the ingredients and the land the ingredients come from.

My love for food runs deep, and with that, so too does my passion for knives and all that they offer and symbolize: being an artisan and transforming raw ingredients into something visually appealing and nourishing for the soul and body. ○

WORDS BY ETHAN KAWASAKI & PHOTOGRAPHS BY ALPHA SMOOT
STYLING BY KENDRA SMOOT

THE COMFORT (FOOD) OF HOME

WORDS BY NICK BAINES & PHOTOGRAPHS BY JAMES BOWDEN

---

*Smack in the center of London's most chaotic area—
where vibrant Chinatown and seedy Soho merge—those seeking
comfort in the form of Japanese staples find whatever their hearts desire
at the Arigato Japanese Supermarket.*

Arigato sits neatly underneath an office block on London's Brewer Street, just a few hundred yards from Piccadilly Circus. The small Japanese supermarket has assumed its place here in Soho, somewhere between the extravagance of theaterland and the raucous, often seedy, seam of the city.

It was a notoriously wet day in London when James and I chose to camp outside the shop, with the sky an oyster gray that cracked sporadically, raining, forcing us to duck into the pub across the street where we sought shelter and a restorative pint. Looking out of that tear-spattered pub window, we watched hurried office workers dash in and out of the unassuming shop doorway, their cargo hidden inside nondescript white carrier bags.

Arigato has long been my go-to place for Japanese ingredients, but on that day I discovered that the shop sells many different things to an incredibly diverse range of people. Beyond the myriad of misos, sake and seaweeds, Arigato offers comfort. For a girl recently migrated from Chiba Prefecture, it comes inside a plastic pot of her favorite brand of instant ramen. For a salesman from the south coast of England, it is a warming meal from the hot-food counter, eaten hungrily at one of the small tables in the corner.

The word "healthy" came up time and again when we spoke to shoppers outside Arigato. Beyond the recipes being followed and the ingredients being procured for experimentation, it became clear that the reasons Arigato's customers were shopping for their Japanese food products were as contrasting as the customers themselves. ○

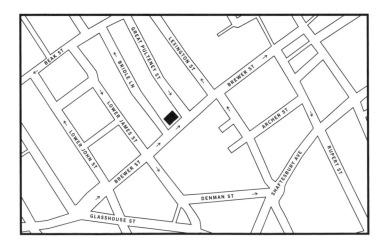

48–50 BREWER STREET, LONDON W1F 9TG

UNITED KINGDOM

NICK TINGLE

Nick Tingle, 24, is studying for a PhD in music. His girlfriend is from Hong Kong and, following a recent trip to see her parents, Nick became enamored with Asian cuisines. He was shopping for a sushi kit and soba noodles.

JOHN WHITE

While in the city on business, aviation marketing executive John White, 56, bought ingredients for his Korean wife back home in Cheltenham.

YUMIKO ISHII

Yumiko Ishii moved to London in 1973 from her home in Tokyo. The 61-year-old shiatsu practitioner regularly shops at Arigato for miso, Bull-Dog sauce and nattō.

CHRIS BOATENG

Chris Boateng is a 28-year-old stylist from southwest London. He had no specific recipe in mind, but wanted to experiment in the kitchen with wasabi powder and seaweed.

STEPHEN MARKESON

Stephen Markeson, 69, is a retired photojournalist for The Times. *"I like to eat healthy, and so I eat a lot of Japanese food," says Stephen. He dropped by for miso soup and wasabi peas.*

MIYA KAO

Miya Kao moved to London five years ago from Taiwan. The 25-year-old sales consultant grabbed shabu-shabu *ingredients to cook a meal for visiting friends.*

LEANDRO FARINA AND NATALIE STOPFORD

Photographer Leandro Farina, 33, and partner Natalie Stopford, a 35-year-old visual-effects producer, visit Arigato regularly to buy ingredients. They stopped in for a lunch of katsudon *and sushi.* ○

WASABI HARVEST

WORDS BY NIKAELA MARIE PETERS & PHOTOGRAPHS BY JULIA GRASSI

A relative of mustard and horseradish, the bright green, sinus-clearing condiment wasabi is generally available as a root or as powder. Here, we share the meticulous process of its production to consumption.

Imagine a wasabi farm as a coral reef above the ocean's surface. Between intricate walls of rocks, green life carpets all available surfaces. The light is indirect, and the air is cool. There is a sense in which a warmer, brighter environment exists miles overhead while the farm abides in a pocket of shadow and fog. The fragile lily pad–shaped leaves act as mini parasols, casting further shade on the rhizome and root structures of the plants.

Every wasabi farmer has his or her distinct method of cultivating and harvesting wasabi. Because the tradition is usually passed within a family from generation to generation, the cultivation and harvest techniques vary by farm. The plant itself might even vary in type from farm to farm, since the environment necessary to grow wasabi is quite specific and the number of farms is limited. Some consistencies remain, however. When the plants flower in the spring they are harvested for seed; the life span of the plant from a seedling to maturity ranges from one and a half to three years; the three-year-old perennials are completely uprooted in the final harvest; the rhizome (which contains the nutrients and flavor) is what is processed to make the spicy condiment commonly eaten with sushi.

Built to simulate the mountain creek beds where the plant is naturally found, wasabi farms are extremely intricate and highly specialized oases. Everything from water temperature to the type and size of stones affects the quality of the crop. The stepped terraces mimic the decline of a mountain river and allow the farmer to control the volume of water that consistently flows over the plants.

Wasabi, like so many elements of Japanese culture, is steeped in tradition, from production to consumption. While most commonly recognized as a condiment eaten alongside sushi (though most of what is served in sushi restaurants and sold in supermarkets is really horseradish dyed green), the plant is far more versatile than its condiment form. When damaged, the plant's built-in defense mechanism responds by releasing strong sulfur compounds, which give wasabi its signature nose-burning, eyes-watering flavor. These same compounds have the ability to "freshen" flavors they're paired with (which is why wasabi takes the "fishy" edge off raw seafood). They also have great health benefits and are being studied by cancer researchers because of their combative nature.

What can we learn from a wasabi farmer? That the old ways are often still the best ways; that building on nature's blueprint can yield the best results; that patience is worthwhile; that secret defenses sometimes protect the strongest flavor. ○

Nikaela Marie Peters lives in Winnipeg, Manitoba, Canada. She is currently completing graduate studies in theology.

JUST THE FLAX: FOG LINEN

*Inspired by the materials that filled her childhood home,
Yumiko Sekine has created Fog Linen, a global empire of simple, durable
and classic linen products to wear and use. We asked her a few questions
to find out how it all came to be.*

INTERVIEW BY SAER RICHARDS & PHOTOGRAPHS BY PARKER FITZGERALD

Some of us fall into our life's vocation by chance; others enter the family business. And there are a few who identify a need and address it with gusto. Yumiko Sekine falls into the latter category; she found her calling through a nostalgia-fueled desire to re-create the linens that filled the family home of her youth. A chance trip to Lithuania more than 10 years ago made that desire a reality.

Yumiko's Fog Linen brand offers a prolific selection of essentials that make a house a home—all created from 100 percent linen. Inspired by the linens her mother used on a daily basis, her collection brims with table napkins in neutral shades and duvets in ginghams reminiscent of summertime school uniforms. It's not surprising to learn that this designer's one-time goal was to be a "happy housewife" since each of her items *feels* like home.

At our initial encounter, I am intrigued that such a quiet and mild spirit as Yumiko could create this exhaustive body of work. Her voice is so gentle, each word seems to be carried on the wind. But her tenacity and courage quickly emerge through her temperateness. And it shows in her work. Every item is flawlessly created and thoughtfully designed to be a part of one's home for decades.

As we chat, I can't help but be enamored by her stories—how determination took her halfway around the world in search of used books, her family's traditions that aren't typically Japanese and how she foresees the legacy of her brand.

TELL US ABOUT YOUR BACKGROUND.

I didn't expect to start my own company. When I was in college, I wanted to be a happy housewife. But when I started working for a housewares store with a cute little café, I really liked it. In time, I was cooking in the café most of the time instead of going to school, and I even helped with the merchandising for the store. That's how I developed an interest in the gift business. However, after finishing college I worked for a furniture company for two years. They sent me to the Philippines to oversee their furniture manufacturing process, to visit furniture design fairs in Europe, as well as gift fairs in the Philippines.

Then I quit my job and worked for a little foreign bookstore for half a year. The store was really small and needed something to attract customers, so I suggested we buy foreign used books to offer something different from the big bookstores. The owners said they didn't want to pay for me to go to other countries to buy books, but that I could do it by myself if I used my own money. I had $3,000 in savings, so bought a ticket to New York and visited various used bookstores. I took my purchases back to Japan and they sold immediately. After that experience I traveled to Portland, Boston, Seattle and other cities to buy books. In time, I got tired of carrying heavy books and my suitcase often broke because they were heavy!

I met someone in San Francisco who was selling wire baskets made in Mexico, and I started to import them. They sold very well in Japan, and I still carry them in my catalog today. From then my business switched to importing gifts instead of books—it was much easier. I could order by fax instead of having to actually go to a store! I started to expand my gift wholesale business to include other items. And then my great-aunt started a Japanese restaurant in Lithuania with her friends.

WAIT, WHERE?

In Lithuania. She had some exchange students from Lithuania stay at her house, but while they were in Japan, Lithuania gained independence from Russia, so they had a difficult time trying to go back to their country. They stayed in Japan for a few years and got to talking about what they could do when they got back home, and somehow started a Japanese restaurant together.

I was curious about Lithuania. However, I didn't find any linen towels at housewares stores when I was there the first time, as people in Lithuania were not using linen products for their daily life; it was more for export.

SO EVEN THOUGH THEY HAD A STRONG HISTORY OF MANUFACTURING LINEN, IT WAS NOW GONE?

They only had linen mostly for export. I could find linen wedding dresses but couldn't find any kitchen towels or aprons at all. Then they told me I could hire the old women to sew things for me, but they didn't have any experience with exporting to Japan, so I was worried. I looked in the phone book and called 10 factories. Most of them didn't understand English and just hung up, but two of them understood. I originally thought I could buy something from them, but then I realized that they didn't have any actual product samples they could show me, but just fabric. I needed to sketch designs and they would make them. That's really how I got started.

YOUR PRODUCTS ARE ALMOST ALL 100 PERCENT LINEN. WHY LINEN?

When I was a child, my mother would use linen tablecloths, napkins and pillowcases at home so it was normal for me to use it. But when I moved to Tokyo for college and was living by myself, I realized linen items were so expensive. I started looking for affordable linen products I could use when I met with the factory in Lithuania and thought I could design them myself.

WHAT THREE THINGS CURRENTLY INSPIRE YOU?

I got inspired by many customers and stores who carry Fog Linen items, especially Julie (my business partner and the owner of the Shop Fog Linen website). She knows how to translate Fog Linen for the US market. I'm inspired when I see how other people use my products. Also, many of my customers inspire me when they tell me what they want and need.

Memories from my childhood: I like the way my mother kept my house. Also, the clothes I wore when I was a child; I still have them and often look at them for inspiration for fabric patterns.

My everyday life: I find ideas from the needs in my life.

DO YOU HAVE ANY PERSONAL TRADITIONS, OR ONES THAT HAVE BEEN PASSED DOWN?

My family likes to welcome foreign friends and guests, like my great-aunt who had the foreign students stay at her house. My parents often did a house exchange with other retirees from France, and my grandmother would also have foreign students stay at her house. Many Japanese people are not so open to having strangers stay in their home, but in my family, we really like it. All these experiences made me feel at ease to travel and work in other countries.

YOUR WORK HAS A TIMELESS QUALITY. WHAT ARE THE THREE KEY ELEMENTS OF FOG LINEN?

Useful, simple and durable. ○

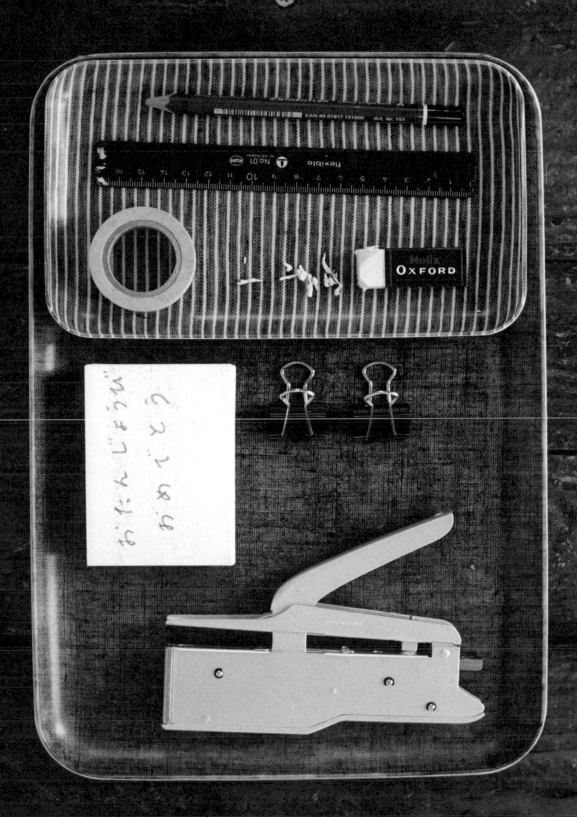

FULL BLOOM: USES FOR CHERRY BLOSSOMS

*Use our guide to make the most of
cherry/sakura blossoms while they last.*

WORDS BY ASHLEY PAQUIN

ILLUSTRATIONS BY KATIE RIDLEY

ADORN

1. Bring branches inside to decorate tables
and hearths.
2. Fill bowls of water with flowers and floating
candles; place outside near the entrance of
your home.
3. Garnish serving platters with smaller cherry
tree branches.

CREATE

1. Hand-tint menus using dye made from
boiling cherry wood.
2. Press blossoms in books, then include in
thank-you cards or handwritten notes.
3. Sew blossoms on gold string and dry over the
mantelpiece, baby's crib or table.

GATHER AND CELEBRATE

1. Have a traditional *hanami*: gather beneath the trees with food and drink to rejoice in the arrival of spring.
2. Visit botanical gardens worldwide and join in the merriment of hanami.
3. Bring the celebration inside with colorful paper lanterns, platters of sakura *mochi* and pots of green tea.

EDIBLES

1. Add blossoms to a green salad to showcase spring's beauty.
2. Enjoy sakura blossom macarons, which are so loved by both the French and Japanese.
3. Use cherry wood to grill or smoke food, imparting a sweet and delicate flavor.
4. Infuse a quarter cup of fine salt with three tablespoons of sakura flowers.
5. Make *onigiri*, Japanese rice balls, and wrap in a preserved and salted cherry leaf.

Note: It is best to gather and use wild-crafted blossoms and branches from their wild, natural habitat. Avoid any plants that may have been exposed to toxic chemicals or pesticides.

IMBIBE

1. Brew delicate white tea and float fresh blossoms on top. Add a touch of cherry blossom honey.
2. Infuse a bottle of sake or vodka with sakura blossoms for seven days, then remove the blossoms to serve.
3. Drink traditional blossom tea, called *sakurayu*, which is fragrant with a slightly salty-sour taste.
4. Enjoy an elderberry spritzer: Shake one ounce of elderberry syrup over ice and top with chilled soda water. Garnish with lemon slices and cherry blossoms. ○

Note: Avoid any plants that may have been exposed to toxic chemicals or pesticides.

CHERRY BLOSSOM MACARONS WITH BLACK SESAME

*Satisfy your inner cookie monster with these tiny, colorful hamburger-shaped treats
that are cuter than Hello Kitty, as well as fluffy and delicious.*

RECIPE & PHOTOGRAPHS BY KATHRIN KOSCHITZKI

s there anything more *kawaii* than a cherry blossom *macaron*? Resembling tiny pink hamburgers, these petite and delightful cookies offer a creamy filling—made with white chocolate, the essence of cherry blossoms and black sesame—sandwiched between super-fluffy meringue-like wafers that melt in your mouth.

Some sources suggest that the French-style macaron dates back to 1533, and after variations have developed in Switzerland, Japan and Korea, these adorable treats have finally been popping up all around the US and Canada in recent years. Make some now for a friend's party, a date with your best friend or just for you. You know you deserve them.

FOR THE FILLING

7 ounces / 200 grams white chocolate, finely chopped

4 ounces / 120 milliliters heavy cream

5 tablespoons (5 ounces / 150 grams) crème fraîche

Cherry blossom essence

Black sesame seeds

FOR THE SHELL

1 cup (4.4 ounces / 125 grams) almond flour, sifted through a very fine sifter

¾ cup plus 2 tablespoons (4.4 ounces / 125 grams) confectioners' sugar

4 medium egg whites (3.1 ounces / 90 grams)

½ cup plus 5 teaspoons (4.4 ounces / 125 grams) granulated sugar

2 tablespoons (1 ounce / 30 grams) water

Food coloring (your favorite rose or violet tone)

FILLING METHOD Place the white chocolate in a medium bowl. Bring the cream to a boil over medium-high heat in a small saucepan and pour it over the chocolate. Allow the mixture to rest for about two minutes, then stir until the mixture is smooth and the white chocolate is completely melted. Allow to cool for about five minutes, then stir in the crème fraîche and a few drops of cherry blossom essence. Cover the bowl with foil and refrigerate it until the mixture thickens.

SHELL METHOD Place the almond flour, confectioners' sugar and half of the egg whites in a large bowl and stir with a rubber spatula until well combined.

Place the remaining egg whites in a clean, dry bowl and fit an electric mixer with the whisk attachment.

In a medium saucepan, bring the sugar and water to a boil over medium-high heat. Cook until the syrup registers 235°F / 113°C on a candy thermometer, at which point you should start beating the whites on medium speed. (They should reach soft peak consistency.) When the syrup reaches 244°F / 118°C, slowly and steadily pour it into the egg whites with the mixer still running. Continue beating until the egg whites turn into stiff, glossy peaks, about three minutes.

Using a rubber spatula, fold a third of the meringue into the almond flour mixture until it is thoroughly combined. Gently fold in the remaining meringue. Add food coloring, folding in after each drop is added (a little goes a long way), until desired color is attained.

Fill a piping bag fitted with a number 10 pastry tip. Line a baking sheet with parchment paper and use some of the batter to anchor the corners down to the sheet. Pipe small dollops of the macaron mixture onto the parchment. If you have small peaks on your shells, carefully tap the baking tray on your kitchen surface and they will disappear.

Adjust an oven rack to the middle position and preheat the oven to 325°F / 165°C. If available, set the oven to convection.

Allow the macarons to rest for 20 minutes to allow them to dry out a bit. To test them, carefully touch them with a fingertip; if they aren't sticky, they are ready to bake.

Bake the macarons for six minutes, open the oven to allow excess steam to escape, rotate the baking sheet, then continue baking for an additional six minutes. Transfer the baking sheet to a cooling rack and cool the macarons completely.

To assemble, fill a piping bag with the white chocolate ganache and dollop a bit on the bottom (flat) side of half of the macarons, then sandwich the remaining halves on top. Roll the edges in black sesame seeds.

Although it is hard to resist, the filled macarons need to rest in an airtight container in the refrigerator for a full day before you eat them. If prepared this way, the moisture of the filling makes the shell as soft as it should be.

Note: While cup measurements are provided in this recipe, a scale to weigh out ingredients is highly recommended. Baking is an exact science, and it is doubly so when making delicate confections such as macarons.

Use high-quality white chocolate for best results. ○

Makes about 30 macarons

BUILDING BLOCKS

The architecture of Tokyo is changing so fast it's hard to keep track. Here, a writer remembers the time he called the city home and notes the changes to his old stomping ground.

Tokyo is huge, washing from horizon to horizon like a great, gray tide; the Greater Tokyo area houses a population almost as big as Canada's. In the five and a half years I lived there, a decade ago, I never got high enough to get a real sense of its size. Despite this enormity, Tokyo is largely low-rise and low-tech; many of its buildings have a simplicity reminiscent of postwar British prefabs or American shotgun houses. Most apartments I lived in were in small, two-story blocks built of wood, a flexible material ideal for building on constantly shifting (occasionally heaving) land. Fire threatens any wooden metropolis with buildings so closely packed that their eaves touch, so when the air is dangerously dry, volunteers take to the streets, knocking wooden blocks together. Their *tok tok tok* reminds residents to be vigilant about stray sparks or popping coals.

These wooden buildings are thrown up or torn down in the space of days, but even more substantial high-rise districts shimmer and reinvent themselves in witness to impermanence. Omotesandō, the city's premier boulevard, is a eulogy to commerce in glass and steel. Dior, Vuitton, Prada, Miyake—each has its temple, but not one of them would be old enough to attend high school. The newest of these epoch-making commercial complexes, Omotesandō Hills, was built in the dust of an ivy-covered, Bauhaus-inspired apartment block. The Dōjunkai Architecture Firm built 16 such iconic apartment complexes in the 1920s and '30s. All survived WWII bombings, but today only one remains, eluding the wrecking ball.

Renewal doesn't always bring about destruction, however. The elegant wooden shrine at Ise, the most sacred site of Shintō, Japan's indigenous religion, is demolished every two decades, its relics moved to an identical replica on an adjacent plot. This year sees the construction and consecration of its 62nd incarnation, faithful in every detail to the original, built 1,220 years ago.

My favorite Tokyo home was a makeshift wooden house in Shirokanedai. I could touch the front and back walls simultaneously, with arms outstretched. The lane it stood on wasn't much wider. I could only fit up the stairs sideways, and the bathroom was the size of a coffin. It was a simple two up, two down; downstairs to the left was the kitchen, to the right my dressmaker landlady's lounge-cum-bedroom. Upstairs on the left, her workroom was piled high with bolts of cloth, while my room was to the right. All my belongings were stowed behind a curtain and the remaining tatami-matted space was just big enough to roll out a futon. Sometimes I invited friends over one at a time. Our knees touched over cups of tea. Lost items were easily found as the house tilted backward: anything that could roll or slide gathered along one wall.

Recently, I searched for the house on Google Street View. With no record of the address, I had only imperfect memory and unreliable landmarks, such as noodle shops and pachinko parlors, to navigate by. I thought I located where it once stood, now a bijou parking lot, and then promptly lost my bearings in the warren of narrow streets. I clicked past a fishmonger and tofu kiosk, and there it was, planks peeling, awkward sliding door still unreplaced. I kept the page open on my laptop for days, in case I was unable to find the house again, but eventually lost it to an uncharged battery.

Tokyo is a city where whole blocks disappear overnight and entire neighborhoods change character like an actor switching costumes. My Tokyo has been all but erased in the years since I left, with favorite haunts giving way to convenience stores and office blocks. That my simple little wooden house endures seems nothing short of miraculous. ○

Richard Aslan is a writer and editor who's interested in how people live, the languages they speak and the food they eat. He's currently based in Bristol, UK, but has also lived in Egypt, Japan, Ecuador and Spain.

WORDS BY RICHARD ASLAN & PHOTOGRAPHS BY WE ARE THE RHOADS

IKEBANA: LEARNING TO BRANCH OUT

Florist Riley Messina demonstrates the quiet, minimal, spiritual process of Japanese flower arranging called ikebana.

WORDS BY RILEY MESSINA & PHOTOGRAPHS BY PARKER FITZGERALD

In the tradition of *ikebana*, an artist combines three elements to represent heaven, Earth and man. The intention to bring forward a greater simplicity in design is first evident when gathering the few materials needed. Using a *kenzan* (pin frog) and a sharp pair of shears, carefully select branches and flowers—often just a few—and manipulate to form harmony in negative space. Essential to the process is a still and contemplative environment. Allow yourself the time to collect foliage, gathering even the bug-eaten blooms as nature intended, and settle into a quiet space to arrange.

---

1. Prepare your container and work area. Place your kenzan in a shallow bowl filled with water; any will do, but a pretty one is best. Clear a comfortable table space and lay out your tools and materials.

2. Gather the goods. Choose branches and flowers of different lengths and textures from your florist or cut a few favorites from the yard. When selecting, think about how the flowers will interact with one another as they are arranged.

3. Arrange. Before putting a stem in water be sure to cut it with a sharp knife at an angle, or use ikebana shears. Place flowers directly into the kenzan at varied angles; the pins will hold the stems in place. Remember to be intentional with each stroke. Simplicity is key. ○

TWO

ENTERTAINING FOR TWO

二人の楽しみ方

○ ○

SLOW AND STEADY: TORTOISE SHOP

WORDS BY JOSH LESKAR & PHOTOGRAPHS BY LOU MORA

Fast food, fast fashion, fast world. Los Angeles creatives Taku and Keiko Shinomoto started Tortoise and Tortoise General Store to combat all that is cheap and quick, and instead focus on quality and longevity.

After more than a decade working in Japan's corporate design industry, Taku and Keiko Shinomoto suddenly became aware of a problem in their surroundings. While humans are living longer, the objects we create are rarely able to keep pace. So when the two married in 2000, they decided to break from their shells, quit their stable full-time jobs with no future plans and embark upon a journey, determined to discover what life had in store.

After two years of traveling around Japan, meeting new people and experiencing nature, the "tortoise life" began to reveal itself to Taku and Keiko. A symbol of longevity, the tortoise takes each day simply as it comes, embodying a grounded and subsequently enriching lifestyle. Slowly, a path began to materialize before the couple until they were finally able to clear their brains and realize precisely "what we needed and wanted for ourselves."

As it turned out, others yearned for the same.

Ever since, the Shinomotos have been operating Tortoise General Store in Los Angeles, a shop dedicated to providing products that reflect the lifestyle of its mascot, offering items of practical simplicity and beauty that are not only crafted by hand, but also with spirit—with a craftsman's pride. Taku and Keiko applied their combined knowledge from previous careers with their personal sense of aesthetic to line the store's shelves with housewares, kitchenware, stationery and books—all crafted with techniques honed throughout centuries of Japanese history—rather than stocking anything trendy. The Shinomotos focus on supplying items that will last for generations to come, and ones that they would want for their own home (making it difficult to choose favorites!).

Taku and Keiko also take pride in educating by offering workshops and events intended to share a piece of Japanese experience and culture with their patrons. In turn, they have immersed themselves in a strong, tight-knit community, of which they are proud to be members. When the biggest earthquake to hit Japan caused unfathomable damage on March 11, 2011, it was the local community that helped Tortoise collect donations for the relief efforts. At that moment, the Shinomotos realized that their customers—their friends—recognize them as more than a source of goods, but also as a source of "real Japan."

Ultimately, their goal is to achieve balance, a passion they have been pursuing for the past 10 years at Tortoise General Store. In both the US and Japan, the tortoise serves as an icon for the slow-and-steady way of life and has, for Taku and Keiko, become a bridge to connect cultures across the Pacific—one craft at a time. ○ ○

A native Floridian, Josh Leskar is a writer, educator and marathon runner. He currently lives, works and plays in San Francisco.

TORTOISE GENERAL STORE: 1208 Abbot Kinney Boulevard, Venice, California
TELEPHONE: 310-314-8448 / WEBSITE: tortoisegeneralstore.com

FUNCTION AND FORM

WORDS BY LOUISA THOMSEN BRITS & PHOTOGRAPHS BY ANAIS & DAX

The tradition of hand dyeing fabric in Japan is a long and respected one. The author walks us through the process here and explains how beauty and durability can coexist.

Every year seeds are sown, plants are grown and harvested and leaves are piled, mixed with sake, wheat bran, ash and lime to ferment a national secret: indigo dye. Woven hemp, ramie, cotton and silk are bound, folded, wrapped, knotted, twisted, pleated, capped and dipped to make *shibori* cloth. Each length of fabric is different, its individuality a gift of the handmade and natural process. With time and air, the colors change from green to the many hues of blue that seem to carry a particular nostalgia and a message most people in Japan still recognize. Indigo cloth has been the fabric of people's lives for hundreds of years, used to make work clothes, futons, floor mats, uniforms, shop signs and banners for temples and shrines.

Laborers, farmers and fishermen once wore hardwearing indigo-dyed cloth to repel snakes and insects. Over time, for protection, warmth and durability, layers of fabric were sewn together with small running stitches to form *sashiko* patterns thought to give spiritual protection: stars, leaves, circles and overlapping arcs for strength and good fortune and abstract images of everyday objects, signs and talismanic patterns to protect the wearer against shipwrecks and evil spirits.

The stories of many families and the forgotten values of *mottainai* (or "too good to waste") can be found in and traced along the stitches, seams and folds of *boro* fabric—cloth pieced together from scraps of old clothes and household items, carefully repaired and handed down from one generation to the next.

Craftsmanship is still passed from aging hands to young. The longevity of craft reminds us that good design has no boundaries. It speaks a universal language that's understood through different generations and cultures all over the world. This is the language of *yo no bi*, or "beauty in utility," the language of things that have both function and a kind of precious commonplace beauty.

The narratives of our lives are inextricably linked by the craft and quality of everyday things; a bowl, stool, mat, rice paddle or piece of clothing that has been made with integrity and treasured for years is eloquent with use and the character that comes from the warmth of human wear.

Continued on page 69

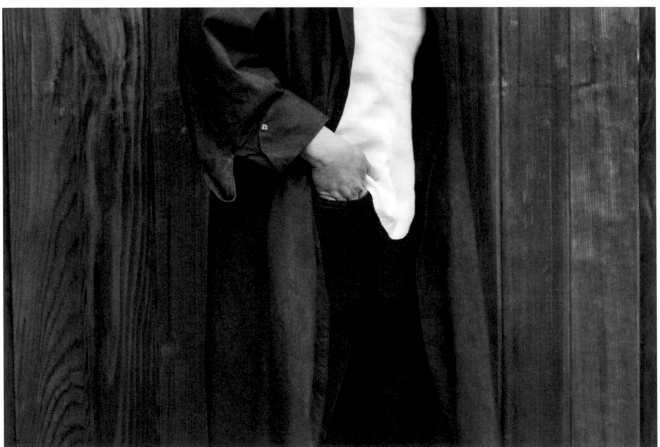

"Indigo cloth has been the fabric of people's lives for hundreds of years, used to make work clothes, futons, floor mats, uniforms, shop signs and banners for temples and shrines"

The honest beauty of the hand-thrown, carved, patched and stitched is born of necessity. At a time when the fingers of recession are spread all over the world, we seem to pay closer attention to the rhythm of domestic life, to the value of small daily rituals and handmade goods that offer us both practical value and comfort; we see the inherent qualities of the objects we use every day and recognize that the indentations and soft curves of a hand-thrown cup can transform a moment from simply mundane to resonant and restorative. A potter knows that a vessel is only complete when it is used.

Japanese craftspeople believe that their work is to give voice to the materials available to them; that craft isn't about an artist simply imposing their own ideas on clay or cotton. Art is inherent in the material itself.

When we discover beauty that was born rather than made, we begin to understand *mingei*—the art of the people; the utilitarian, familiar, affordable, accessible craft that gives depth to our daily lives. Mingei shines light on what once may have seemed ubiquitous and dull. It expresses our universal, instinctive response to the comfort of practicality, asymmetry and natural form. It reminds us of the essential marriage of history, narrative, necessity, skill and heart.

When we keep the cycle of craft alive, we reach far back in order to move forward. When we make, buy or give something that has drawn its context and process from the wisdom of our immediate environment, we experience a deeper engagement with life and sense a connection to something that's higher than our selves. Maybe if we pause to consider how we live, create and consume, we will savor things that have been made in a spirit of generosity and resourcefulness, in close harmony with nature. And we will place more value on those who are prepared to plant the seeds and maintain an environment where new growth can take place and the life of craft can flourish. ○○

Louisa Thomsen Brits is a writer, mother of four, tribal belly-dance teacher and novice coffee roaster. She lives in rural East Sussex, United Kingdom.

HAND DYE COORDINATION

WORDS BY KATIE SEARLE-WILLIAMS & PHOTOGRAPHS BY ANAIS & DAX

In Japan, the *shibori* technique dates back to the eighth century. Indigo, a natural chemical extracted from plants, is one of the oldest organic dyes used for coloring cloth and is most commonly used for shibori. Indigo dye must be applied to natural fibers and clothes that have not been treated with any finishes nor blended with synthetic, man-made materials. The deep hue of indigo is ideal for creating contrasting resist patterns on light-colored fabrics. The exploration of patterns, combined with the meditative process of indigo dyeing, is a rewarding pastime.

100% natural fabrics, clothing or yarn to dye

Rubber bands or string and small pieces of wood to make patterns

Latex gloves (preferably long)

20 grams (.7 ounces) pre-reduced indigo (available in most indigo dye kits)

250 grams (9 ounces) reducing agent (available in most indigo dye kits)

Five-gallon (19 liters) bucket for dye bath

A long stick to gently move items in the bath

Tray or flat sheet of wood for oxidation process

Laundry rack and clothespins for drying

Mild soap (like Woolite) and plain white vinegar to set the dye

Five-gallon (19 liters) bucket for water/vinegar rinse

1) Dampen your fabric with water and choose one or more of the following shibori techniques: bind, tie or twist with rubber bands or string, or compress and pleat using small pieces of wood and rubber bands.

2) Put on latex gloves and follow the indigo dye kit directions to prepare the dye bath in a five-gallon bucket.

3) Gently dip your shibori-prepared fabric all the way into the indigo dye bath; do not splash. Stir gently using a long stick.

4) Pull fabric out slowly up the side of the vat to avoid drips. Your fabric will be a yellow-green color when it emerges from the bath for the first time. Place fabric on a tray in the open air and allow all parts of the fabric to oxidize to the color blue (turn fabric over for full oxidation). Once all is oxidized to blue, let sit for 20 minutes and then repeat steps three and four for darker shades of indigo.

5) Dip at least three times for a medium shade of indigo and up to eight to ten times for a deeper shade. The fabric will look very dark when wet.

6) Rinse the fabric with water and undo the shibori bindings to reveal the intricate patterns created.

7) Hang the dyed fabric on a laundry rack and let rest overnight.

8) Conclude with a final rinse of the dyed fabric with a small amount of mild soap (about 1/2 small cap). Mix tap water (two gallons) and a small amount of plain white vinegar (1/3 cup) in a five-gallon bucket, and set the dyed fabric in this bath for at least five minutes.

9) Wash separately.

10) Enjoy. ○ ○

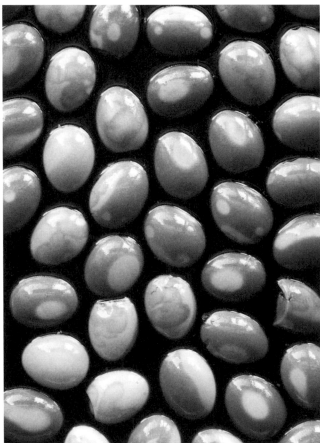

STOCK IN TRADE

WORDS BY AYA MUTO & PHOTOGRAPHS BY ERIN KUNKEL — STYLING BY LISA MOIR

Oakland's Ramen Shop has quickly become a favorite stop for anyone who likes their noodles and broth made with tons of flavor, imagination and carefully chosen ingredients.

Broth made from house-dried sardines, hand-roasted nori seaweed harvested on the coast of Mendocino, freshly foraged oyster mushrooms and dried chilies flaked in house for the touch of sweetness the local varietal offers: these are the details that go into each bowl of Ramen Shop's noodle soup. Jerry Jaksich, Sam White and Rayneil De Guzman—the partners behind this Oakland eatery— are graduates of Chez Panisse, Alice Waters' restaurant in Berkeley, and have applied their passion for local, seasonal ingredients to the humble meal that Japan continues to renovate with passion.

Ramen is an adaptation from Chinese cuisine, to which Japan applied its own twist. It is made with regional specialty broth; some combination of items—be it seaweed, fish, chicken or pork bones—is cooked for up to several days in a big pot. Ratios of blends are rarely used twice. Noodle texture and thickness are their own journey, too. You'll always have the option of walking into a ramen shop on any city street in Japan, while food magazines like to feature ramen several times a year.

When the ramen bowl is served, the meal often happens quickly. "Ramen is a solitary meal," explains Jaksich, who spent six years in Japan teaching English and conducting ramen research. "Most of the ramen shops consist of just a counter, some with a refined system where a customer orders through a machine and hands the ticket over the counter. No room for any mistakes to be made, super efficient." His first meal in Japan was a bowl of ramen that brought him a complete epiphany. From then on, he spent much of his free time finding the perfect soup, visiting, working and even apprenticing at a regional Italian fine dining restaurant in a remote town in Japan, learning all aspects of culinary ways. When he returned to the US, he wanted to work at Chez Panisse.

While Jaksich is the force behind the ramen, De Guzman brings more than 10 years of culinary experience to the table. By the time its doors opened officially in January 2013, Ramen Shop had been perfecting every detail—from broth to noodle, from garnishes to pop-up events. White co-founded a situational art-food gathering called Open, and Ramen Shop was also involved. After Japan suffered the earthquake and the unfortunate incidents following it, the Open collective was quick to join the mission to help the Bay Area's food community support Japan.

Some key ingredients, such as fermented bonito flakes, are imported from Japan, and sometimes, Ramen Shop uses its resources and experiences to come up with better alternatives. "Rayneil suggested Roman-style deep-fried artichoke to go on top as a substitute to *menma* [pickled/fermented bamboo shoots, a trademark ramen topping] because I had a hard time sourcing the good quality ones," says Jaksich. "The texture and flavor I was explaining just prompts Rayneil with different culinary ideas, and it's fantastic. Our menu changes every day, and it's always ingredient-oriented." There is also one bowl available for vegetarians.

As White prints out the day's menu after the staff meeting where Jaksich and De Guzman explain the art and story behind all the ingredients and preparation, people are starting to form a line outside. The counter—made by a woodworker friend with reclaimed wood from Oregon—is fresh and fragrant, and White and his bartenders are preparing to serve local distillery–made *shochu* and other cocktails, to make the waiting experience exciting. The boiling of noodles, which are prepared daily, happens in front of your eyes if you sit at the counter, and vegetables, braised pork and precooked eggs will perfect the appearance of the bowl. In Oakland, the bowl of ramen represents a gathering of multiple communities, on both sides of the counter. ○ ○

RAMEN SHOP: 5812 College Avenue, Oakland, California / TELEPHONE: 510-788-6370
WEBSITE: ramenshop.com

KEEPING TIME

WORDS BY REBECCA PARKER PAYNE

The concepts of ichi-go ichi-e *and* mono no aware *show us how to focus on the here and now and appreciate the ones we're with.*

It is Monday night, and it is late. My mind is occupied by tomorrow's work, but my sister sits in front of me and she is asking me to talk. In a deeper way, she's asking me to be with her and I cannot say no. So we talk, far into the darkest hours of this arbitrary Monday night. But this is our time.

Japanese tradition tells of *ichi-go ichi-e*, a concept fortified over centuries of practice that says we only have one meeting, at one time—our experiences with one another stand alone. Every encounter we have—a dinner, a shared bottle of wine, a late evening of conversation on an old red couch—will happen once, and then will never happen again. The circumstances surrounding an encounter, the people involved and their exact dispositions and history make each event unique. We may interact with the same people, within similar circumstances, but ichi-go ichi-e says that each interaction is an experience all unto itself, never to be re-created perfectly.

This concept is often used to describe the famous Japanese tea ceremony. An artistic display of both hospitality and decorum, the tea ceremony demands vigilant preparation, as well as keen attention to the practice of being present. The host's aim is to garner a high level of mindfulness and intention for the event, but once the event begins, she must be acutely aware of what is happening. This is the host's time to be here fully and to be with her friends and loved ones.

Ichi-go ichi-e reminds us to be mindful, but also to be present, so we may be moved by the natural combination of factors at play in any moment: people, food on the table, the weather outside. In traditional Japanese Noh theater, actors only rehearse a few times before a performance, so the authentic interactions of the performers, along with the natural combination of factors present at that moment, will move the performance. Even in theater, an art where scripted rehearsal is typically of the utmost importance, the Japanese remind us to relinquish control.

Ichi-go ichi-e holds both the purposefulness of preparation and the spontaneity of presence in perfect equilibrium. The culture I know and live within often celebrates polarity. We are stalwarts of the extremes, either holistically spontaneous or absolutely controlled. And it is the Japanese who remind us that spontaneity and intentionality are not mutually exclusive but become more necessary within the light of the other.

Relinquishing control in my day-to-day existence does not involve a tea ceremony or improvisational acting, but the concept is relevant enough: I relinquish my internal script when I host friends in my home, relinquish my plans of going to bed early when an important conversation arises instead. For me, ichi-go ichi-e looks strangely similar to working hard and also letting go. And it makes complete sense, as if that's the way all hospitality should be—purposefulness mingled with whimsy.

—

Furthermore, Japanese understand this concept within another framework called *mono no aware*. Literally translated as "the pathos of things," mono no aware is the understanding that the most beautiful moments of life come right before the moment ends. In a full acceptance of the transient and temporal state of life, the Japanese don't hold much appreciation for an eternally blossoming flower. Instead, the greater beauty comes within the constraints of our yearly life and death rhythms. Mono no aware calls us to sit below the cherry blossoms as the tree sheds its blooms. It tells us not to lament the passing of summer, but to rejoice in its final hours.

We are creatures capable of awe and reverence. And we can position our selves and our hearts to feel heavy and wonderful things. But to choose to see the beauty in the passing is no easy task. We must first cast off our illusions of control, and then we must take a step back and prepare ourselves for the full spectrum of pathos—love, beauty, loss. Perhaps then we will see all the gold that doesn't stay as beautiful instead of defeatist.

Mono no aware tells us to love now. Act now. Be here now. Invite our friends over, and stay up late. Because this time, this opportunity, this season will soon pass. Bask here while it is still possible.

Our days are ebbs and flows. Our lives are a collection of seasons where tides approach and recede, and trees flower and wither. The green fullness of summer is made more precious by the skeleton branches of winter. So don't fight time and don't fight the season. Don't keep things from ending, but celebrate them for the life they have now.

Our lives are rife with endings—the close of an evening or the triumphant finality of summer's last stand. If we reorient our hearts to accept and appreciate these endings, we begin to see our lives outside our limited terms—not only for our wanton control and desires, but also for mankind as a whole. Time is not ours. We can't slow the Earth's rotation, and we can't expect a wedding celebration to last forever.

I want to respect that which is larger than me—the sun that rises in the East and sets in the West, the gravity that keeps my feet perpetually on the ground below and the rhythm of time that says to all creation: this too shall pass.

—

So I find myself on this old red couch, my young sister's big brown eyes peeking up at me from behind her glasses, asking me to talk with her. On this night where I expected to eat soup, watch a movie and go to bed at a decent hour, we talk. We talk well past my planned bedtime, and then well past midnight. I invited her into my home, and my rehearsed plans for the evening evaporated—because who we were and where we were on this night demanded a long conversation, and because we will soon outgrow this season of her crashing on my couch on any arbitrary Monday night.

I can't budget for time like this. I do my best to prepare, putting my heart where it needs to be, but I can't rehearse it or perfect it. So much of life happens outside of our expectations and our preparedness. So much of life does not look perfect. I'm far from perfect: eyes dark, makeup long gone and any sort of style replaced by wool socks and my husband's sweater. This does not look like perfection, but it does look a lot like being completely here, in this moment, with her.

Because she is here now, in my living room, and in the morning she'll be gone. This is our one meeting, one time. It might be one out of a million like these, but it stands alone if I let it. And because she will leave for school in the morning, and I'll go to work, our time now is that much sweeter. So as the hours wane and our conversation draws to a close, we rest in an evening fulfilled. In these last few minutes, we could not be closer, even though we are seconds from parting ways.

It is here that these ancient concepts converge. It is the ichi-go ichi-e and it is the mono no aware in perfect tandem: one meeting, one time within the beauty of the temporal. With these traditions, we are engaged unto the end, because we have been made present from the beginning. ○○

Rebecca Parker Payne is a writer from Virginia, where she bakes pies, drinks bourbon and spins old bluegrass on vinyl with her husband. She writes about all things concerning food, family, community and place.

OLD LIVES TALES

*Keep calm and carry these Japanese proverbs close at hand
to live well and gain wisdom.*

PHOTO ESSAY BY HIDEAKI HAMADA & TRANSLATIONS BY MASAFUMI KAJITANI

*Hideaki Hamada is a photographer based in Osaka, Japan. Born in 1977
in Hyogo, he is the father of Haru and Mina (pictured).*

雨降って地固まる
(ame futte ji katamaru)

LITERALLY: After the rain, earth hardens.
MEANING: Adversity strengthens the foundations. / After a storm, things
will stand on more solid ground than they did before.

十人十色
(*jūnin toiro*)

LITERALLY: ten men, ten colors
MEANING: To each his/her own. / Different strokes for different folks.

三日坊主

(mikka bōzu)

LITERALLY: a monk for just three days
MEANING: giving up easily

雲散霧消

(*unsan mushō*)

LITERALLY: scattered clouds, disappearing mist
MEANING: disappear without a trace

二兎を追う者は一兎をも得ず

(nito wo ou mono wa itto wo mo ezu)

LITERALLY: One who chases after two hares won't catch even one.
MEANING: Trying to do two things at once will make you fail in both.

花鳥風月

(kachō fūgetsu)

LITERALLY: flower, bird, wind, moon
MEANING: the beauties of nature

虎穴に入らずんば虎子を得ず

(koketsu ni irazunba koji wo ezu)

LITERALLY: If you do not enter the tiger's cave, you will not catch its cub.
MEANING: Nothing ventured, nothing gained. / You can't achieve anything without risking something.

ごにゅうえん ○ おめでとう

出る杭は打たれる
(deru kui wa utareru)

LITERALLY: The stake that sticks out gets hammered down.
MEANING: Don't make waves. / It's better to conform than to stick out.

言わぬが花

(iwanu ga hana)

LITERALLY: Not speaking is the flower.
MEANING: Silence is golden. / Some things are better left unsaid. ○○

WABI-SABI PEACE

WORDS BY LOUISA THOMSEN BRITS

Late summer is an ideal time to amble down the path of wabi-sabi, *the Japanese concept of appreciation and acceptance of imperfection and impermanence. Louisa Thomsen Brits acts as our guide.*

We step across the doorstep washed by summer rain and into the cool, spare kitchen. The room smells of wood soap and freshly baked cake. On the tabletop, a peony droops its heavy head over the rim of a milk bottle. A single white petal has fallen to the floor. Three small ceramic cups wait on a wooden tray.

"These are the last three I have left—I've drunk my tea from them for almost 50 years," says our neighbor as he smiles and lifts the teapot to pour for us. One end of the wooden handle has uncurled where it meets the smooth curve of the lid. His hands are veined and mottled brown from many morning hours spent tending the community garden. Time stands still and expands as each cup is filled. Steam rises. A distant car door slams. A crow calls.

Like rests between musical notes, there is space here between each moment, each object. On the windowsill is a row of small treasures: a hag stone, a carved wooden box, a tiny rat vertebra, a blue-gray flint, a slender candlestick. Folded linen tea towels hang above the oven to dry.

My son climbs onto my lap. We have come here to slow down, to let go of the disappointments of a scraped knee, a lost toy, an unwieldy tool, an insurmountable task. The door is left open to friendship, sidling cats and evening air.

These are the bittersweet moments we savor: our old friend's open invitation, his warmth and restraint, a welcome at the gate, the cobbled path, the stillness of late afternoon, the presence of lengthening shadows and the knowledge that nothing lasts forever.

I feel the pith and pitch of life, its intangible essence, its fleeting loveliness and acknowledge its inevitable passing like the shadow that slides slowly across the kitchen wall, cast by the evening sun.

We cradle the clay cups and pause, conscious of their rough, worn surface, of the many conversations they have heard. I feel the touch of the potter's hands. Each cup is different, alive with history and imperfection. In each one, we hold a subtle charge and know the gift of *wabi-sabi* like a kiss that endows everything with spirit.

Wabi-sabi is everywhere in this modest, peaceful home where all the inessentials have been pared away. Grass, ivy and the inexhaustible variety of life run right up to the wooden porch. Inside, there is natural harmony, simplicity, order and ease. This is a place of muted tones, texture, mystery, shadow and intangible charm. A rich life is lived here, a life of nuance and flow. The open windows frame a walnut tree that stands alone in the garden. We find ourselves touched by a kind of serene melancholy that comforts and inspires us to look within and gaze beyond. We hear bicycles and bright laughter on the street outside. Our neighbor lights a candle. In a low bowl, there's a handful of unearthed potatoes and fresh dill, picked for the evening meal.

On this small patch of our busy street, each passing season, each cycle of growth and decay and each one of us is welcome. We know that here our flaws are as celebrated as our achievements. Our fragility and our capacity for joy is the thread that ties all our disparate lives together. At this table, we don't have to shine brilliantly, compete or pretend. We are offered both context and freedom—and another piece of date and walnut cake. It's still warm. A small hand reaches for the last slice.

Somewhere, between my child's appetite and joie de vivre and this elderly man's generosity and stillness, is the path of wabi-sabi. It comes with the gift of time and the patina of age to lead us to celebration of imperfection and impermanence. Wabi-sabi reveals the value of the humble, worn and treasured. It teaches us to strip away excess and embrace the unaffected beauty of the moment. It's an invitation to consider a life free from the pursuit of perfection, from the fear of losing the gloss of youth, of not having enough.

When we come here, we learn to weave wabi-sabi into the fabric of our everyday life. We shed self in favor of openness, modesty and authenticity. We remember that enjoying a cup of tea together is a step toward peace and that grace arrives to inhabit the space that we keep swept and clear. Wabi-sabi holds moments of longing and connection, harnesses them to simple objects and everyday activities, infusing them with spirit and illuminating their natural integrity.

Wabi-sabi is this place that's free of greed. It's this man who sees the beauty of rust and peeling paint, who understands the wisdom of rocks, beeswax polish, driftwood and beetles. He shows us that wabi-sabi is a way of seeing, a way of being in the world. It is dry leaves, wooden spoons, washing hung to dry in the wind, worn leather, wild flowers, cotton and careful attention.

Through wabi-sabi we can find a way to live in harmony with nature and trust the natural order of things. We can let go of unrestrained materialism, live lightly on the earth and learn how to inhabit our homes with care and treat each other with equanimity.

Our friend carefully brushes the cake crumbs onto a slate for the birds and washes each plate. My son hops about from one leg to the other, offering to help. A cup slips to the floor and shatters.

"Ah well," the old man says, stooping to pick up a piece and put it on the windowsill. "Don't worry. Nothing lasts forever. And it has been such a pleasure to have your company this evening."

He moves slowly to collect the broom that props open the kitchen door. For a moment, he seems to be simply a part of the flux of dust and light that flow in and out of this house every day. We cherish him and the beauty that exists in that brief time between the coming and going of life. ○○

FEW

ENTERTAINING FOR A FEW

幾人かの楽しみ方

○ ○ ○

EVER-BLOOMING BLOSSOMS

WORDS BY ASHLEY SCHLEEPER & PHOTOGRAPHS BY KATHRIN KOSCHITZKI

Cherry blossom season is fast and fleeting.
Use our instructions to make your own origami paper sculptures
to keep things floral all year round.

Cherry blossoms erupt for but an instant before they pass. Ephemeral to a fault, *sakura*, as they are referred to in Japan, erupt in full bloom then patter offstage like a ballerina. One of the loveliest aspects of sakura is their tendency to grow en masse. No blossom is an island. Rather, buds flower on top of one another, forming a gentle tangle of petals that resembles tufts of clouds, kissed with pink. Beneath these branches of florets, picnickers often gather for a nibble and a bit of banter, a practice known as *hanami*. Unfortunately, the season for hanami is fleeting, not unlike the blossoms themselves.

As synonymous with Japanese culture as sakura, origami—the art of paper folding—stands to right nature's trickery (the swift cherry blossom season). Here are some steps to bend and crease and fold breath into paper flowers that will continue to bloom little by little, as you open only a few blossoms each passing day. These delicate flowers do not require much, save for a bit of patience. Ingredients to have on hand include small bowls for watercolors, a pair of scissors and very thin (about 30g) soakable paper—a crucial agent in the process. Before opening each petal, take care to allow them to dry completely. This is the key to ever-blooming sakura, and an everlasting hanami.

MIRACLE WEED: WAKAME HARVEST

We went to the tiny island of Shinojima to find out how generations of families have learned the craft of getting seaweed out of the ocean and on to our plates.

WORDS BY SAWAKO AKUNE WITH HITOMI THOMPSON & PHOTOGRAPHS BY PARKER FITZGERALD

The men meet on the dark jetty before dawn. The road to the bay is illuminated only by streetlamps, far apart as though they have been forgotten. It is 5 a.m. The men wear thick work clothes and rubber bibs that reach their chests for the final layer. Each wraps a hand towel neatly around his neck, and tucks it under his collar. The wakame season is short. When the men are ready, they get on a small boat and row out to the ocean.

Akikado Tsuji lives and works on an island, Shinojima, in Aichi Prefecture. The Tsuji family farms wakame, makes *tsukudani* and fishes for sardines and whitebait. If one asks in Tokyo where Shinojima is, most would not know. That is how small the island is. It's about an hour and a half by train and boat from Nagoya, headquarters of Toyota and the third largest city in Japan. The island is barely six miles in circumference, and is nestled halfway between the ends of the Chita and Atsumi peninsulas.

Many of the 2,000 or so people that live on the island were born in Shinojima; they grow up there and then take up the family business. Tsuji is one of them. He was born here, and he grew up with the girl who became his wife. They started a family together.

The fishermen on this morning outing are Tsuji, his two sons and nephews. The wakame farm is on the other side of the island from the jetty. They find a tiny marker on the surface of the dark water, and approach slowly, so they do not damage the ropes the wakame is growing on. Once everybody is in a straight line, they gather around the rope and lift the growing wakame, each line carefully, gathering the harvest of the day by hand.

The sun rises and the men are still on the ocean, as though they are carrying the sunlight on their backs as they work. The harvested, slick wakame shines in the basket.

The wakame, once taken to the harbor, is prepared for market. This process is not performed by machines. The shiny brown wakame is blanched in a great big pot that turns it bright green. Next, the women process each one manually. One hand holds a piece of wakame, and the other wields a knife, separating it into the leaves and stems.

The soft, leafy part is the wakame we know well, and is often sold dried. The crunchy stem produces a viscosity when thinly sliced, and tastes great as is.

Wakame, often an ingredient used in miso soup, can also go in salads or vinegary *sunomono*. It can be cooked with rice to add natural, salty flavor to the rice. There is always a place for wakame on the Japanese dining room table, which would be lonely without it. Despite that fact, most people don't know how much of the wakame cultivating and cooking process is done by hand.

Mayumi Nishimura, who is well known for having been a longtime personal chef to Madonna, and who introduced the singer to her macrobiotic diet, is from Shinojima. Mayumi says of the Tsujis that they "were friends before we could speak."

The islands are close in distance to the mainland Honshu, but if the weather and the seas are rough, the island can be unreachable for days. This reality has instilled a self-sufficient lifestyle in the island's inhabitants that remains today. Nature's gifts from the ocean are collected by hand and carefully prepared in order to be cooked and joyfully eaten, becoming a part of your body. There is no mistaking where Mayumi's philosophy has its roots.

The wakame plant that was harvested and prepared by the hands of the Tsuji family is cooked and served by Mayumi. The aroma of the ocean that drifts from the wakame seems strong and thick, satisfying the senses. ○○○

WAKAME CUCUMBER SALAD

RECIPE BY MAYUMI NIIMI & PHOTOGRAPHS BY PARKER FITZGERALD

Wakame is a variety of dried seaweed. Look for it in the international aisle of the supermarket, in Asian markets or in natural food markets. Mirin is a Japanese rice wine found in the international aisle of most supermarkets.

---

1 cup (about 1 ounce / 30 grams) dried wakame seaweed

½ teaspoon (0.1 ounce / 3 grams) sea salt

2-inch (5-centimeter)-long (about 1.5 ounces / 45 grams) seedless cucumber, sliced into thin rounds

¼ cup (2 ounces / 60 milliliters) brown rice vinegar

2 tablespoons (1 ounce / 30 milliliters) maple syrup

1 teaspoon (0.17 ounces / 5 milliliters) soy sauce

1 tablespoon (0.5 ounces / 15 milliliters) mirin (optional)

2 tablespoons (0.7 ounces / 20 grams) toasted sesame seeds

A few drops of toasted sesame oil (optional)

METHOD 1. Reconstitute dried wakame by placing it in a bowl and covering with cold water. Allow to soak until softened, about 15 minutes and up to overnight.

2. Meanwhile, sprinkle the salt over the cucumber slices and allow to sit in a strainer for 10 minutes. Pat dry with paper towels.

3. Drain wakame and squeeze out excess water, then cut into bite-size pieces.

4. Combine the brown rice vinegar, maple syrup, soy sauce and (optional) mirin in a small saucepan and simmer on medium heat for two to three minutes until slightly reduced. Remove from heat, transfer to a medium bowl and cool to room temperature.

5. Add the wakame, cucumber, sesame seeds and (optional) sesame oil to bowl and toss to combine. Serve. ○○○

Serves 4

TREE TO TEA: THE LIFE OF LEAVES

WORDS BY JOSH LESKAR & PHOTOGRAPHS BY JULIA GRASSI

*Japanese green tea farmers put a great deal of art, thought,
patience and care into creating and consuming their product—
from growing the first leaf to the tea-drinking rituals.*

In the life of green tea, a beautiful dichotomy exists. A tea farmer must practice patience, working tirelessly for months to prune, trim and shape each tree, preparing it for its ultimate destiny. After all, when a tea tree is properly maintained, it can gift its bounty for 30 to 50 years, making it indeed worthy of such love and care. Yet this lengthy, tedious process builds to but a single moment in time when suddenly hours, or even precious minutes, can determine the outcome of countless hours of labor.

From seedling infancy, the *Camellia sinensis* is first required to mature anywhere from three to five years before its leaves have developed thoroughly enough to be deemed worthy of plucking. The plant may grow to be nearly 50 feet when left to its own devices: an unruly toddler scampering across the plantation floor, grasping for every object in its path. The tea farmer grooms the growth to a manageable height, teaching it to branch out along a horizontal plane and forcing it to create a flat "picking table" for the harvest ahead.

Sloping hillsides high atop mountain ranges lend ideal conditions for growing the most coveted tea, offering ample amounts of permeable soil through which water can pass while simultaneously preserving sufficient moisture in which the tree thrives. The mountainous terrain also allows the tree's roots to grasp firmly into deep, nutrient-dense terroir.

However, these high altitudes also bring with them extremely challenging climatic variations. The sun's rays grace the leaves by day and yield to breaths of chill evening air, inducing stress and stunting growth. Miraculously, the tree's resilience takes advantage of this adversity and emerges with stronger, fuller and more flavorful leaves as it fights to retain chlorophyll stores, instinctively battling for survival. Often, farmers will even cover the plants in the weeks leading up to the harvest in order to facilitate a similar reaction, causing them to defend against impending damage. Tea trees must live

Continued on page 108

"The Japanese have made the consumption of green tea an art form,
a ceremony to be cherished, respected and treasured leisurely"

their lives in constant flux between struggle and safety.

At long last, picking day finally arrives: one single, perfect day, during the earliest whispers of spring, when a clear blue sky peeks out from beneath winter's gray and when the nutrients rush from the roots to nourish weather-worn leaves, having spent the past season sleeping beneath a blanket of fog and mist, awakening in the nick of time to realize their tender, juicy, ripe potential.

The *shincha*—the first new tea.

Act too soon and the yield may be sparse and the flavors underdeveloped; too late, and the tea's quality may already be compromised. Under the grueling sun overhead, workers toil with nimble precision for hours on end, taking only the outermost two leaves for their intense taste, before carting their haul hurriedly back to the tea house.

The farmer must proceed with haste. From the moment the leaves are extracted from their homes, their biological clock begins ticking backward. Air immediately jeopardizes the tea's very existence as the enzymes thrust into action and oxidation begins to take hold. Quickly, the leaves are steamed over bamboo baskets, halting deterioration in its tracks and locking in the signature green color and grassy, vegetal composition.

In the same manner as a winemaker, the tea producer now becomes an artist. The steaming process can last anywhere from 20 to 120 seconds, every one of which imparts a slightly different flavor profile on the finished product. Once completed, this *aracha* is typically sold off to producers who complete the drying and shaping process; very few tea farmers today see the entire process from start to finish. They must send their product—their offspring—into the world, knowing it will fulfill its mission in life.

The Japanese have made the consumption of green tea more than just that—it is an art form, a ceremony to be cherished, respected and treasured leisurely. Yet for those few hours, from picking to processing, the peace and tranquility that once characterized the entire lifespan of those leaves vanishes, only to be realized once again inside the steaming hot mugs shared among family and friends. ○ ○ ○

MATCHA

RECIPE AND FOOD STYLING BY DIANA YEN, THE JEWELS OF NEW YORK

STYLING ASSISTANTS SUSANNA MOLLER, KALI SOLACK & PHOTOGRAPH BY SETH SMOOT

The transformation of green tea leaves into *matcha* requires a gentle hand and the skill of an artisan. The leaves designated for matcha are supple and protected by shade until their time comes to be plucked from the bush. Harvesters flatten the leaves like lily pads and bathe them in the sun until they are dry and the edges begin to crumble. Once the stems and the veins are removed, the broken bits of leaves are then stone ground into a powder, fine and sweet and brilliantly green. Whisked into steaming water, matcha is often sipped during Zen ceremonies in Japanese monasteries—a splendid tradition to share with friends who have gathered to watch an afternoon laze by.

Matcha bowl or other small bowl

Matcha scoop

Small bamboo whisk

Matcha green tea powder

METHOD Warm the matcha bowl by filling it with enough hot water so that it is about a third full. Rotate and gently shake the bowl to evenly heat it. Warm the tips of the whisk by dipping them in the bowl. Discard the water and thoroughly dry the bowl with a dishcloth.

Measure out 2 scoops (about 3/4 teaspoon / 0.25 ounce / 7 grams) of matcha powder and sift it into the preheated bowl.

Heat water until very hot but not boiling, then pour it over the matcha powder until the bowl is about a third full.

With the bowl in one hand and the whisk in the other, begin to whisk the matcha with your wrist. Move the whisk back and forth in the bowl until a thick froth forms. Serve.

Note: Matcha is a finely milled, high-quality green tea. If it has any clumps, work it through a fine-mesh sieve to break them up. Lightweight ceramic matcha bowls are traditionally used in Japanese tea ceremonies. Bowls and the small bamboo whisks commonly used to prepare the tea can be purchased at specialty stores, especially those carrying exotic teas. ○ ○ ○

Serves 1

SOUL FOOD

WORDS BY ISAAC BESS (WITH KAORU HUDACHEK) & PHOTOGRAPH BY ERIN KUNKEL

In the US, comfort food is melted cheese.
In the UK, it means tea and toast. What is comfort food in Japan?
A former Tokyo resident and his friends weigh in.

In 1986, I moved from New York to Japan with my family. Even though I've been in San Francisco for a million years now, I stay connected with my extended Tokyo family. A bunch of us still get together to cook and eat every week here in California, and they were the first ones I reached out to when Japanese comfort food came up.

At first I figured we could break it out, a tidy little guide citing well-known classics such as おでん (humble fish cake stew), 唐揚げ (fried chicken), even オムライス (rice omelet, lots of ketchup) or ピザまん (Chinese pork bun with "pizza" swapped in for pork, the original Hot Pocket)—stuff anyone's mom might make or any kid could grab from a convenience store.

I also thought of a dish called ハンバーグ *("hanbaagu")*—not to be confused with ハンバーガー *("hanbaagaa")*—which is a postwar fave that took the Japanification of the lowly hamburger to wild new heights, adding pork, replacing ketchup with demi-glace (!) and doing away entirely with the bun. It's now served at "family restaurants" such as Royal Host or Jonathan's, so any airs of sophistication have been replaced by the nostalgia of being 10 and living in the Yokohama 'burbs.

Okay, fine, but ハンバーグ has probably been documented to death already. It's a bit like saying SpaghettiOs is comfort food. So I put it back to the group, and of course a *huge* email debate ensued—comfort food is really controversial! Have you ever watched two Germans argue about whether or not potato salad should have caraway seeds? Heated! At any rate, after an extremely long email thread, the best response came from my dear friend Kaoru, whose recipe for, well, raw egg topped them all.

"生卵 [raw egg]—we used to crack it, and mix it with 醤油 [soy sauce] and 味の素 [ajinomoto, a.k.a. delicious MSG] and pour it over ごはん [plain white rice]," says Kaoru. "Eat it with のり [dried seaweed] that's dipped in 醤油 [more soy]. Mmm, pour 納豆 [gooey, stinky fermented soybeans / nattō] on it. That's the ultimate comfort food!" ○○○

Isaac Bess has flitted around the independent music world in New York, Tokyo and San Francisco for nearly 20 years now.

GLOSSARY

FISH CAKE STEW	おでん
FRIED CHICKEN	唐揚げ
RICE OMELET	オムライス
PIZZA BUN, THE ORIGINAL HOT POCKET	ピザまん
HAMBURGER STEAK	ハンバーグ
REGULAR OLD HAMBURGER	ハンバーガー
RAW EGG	生卵
SOY SAUCE	醤油
AJINOMOTO A.K.A. MSG	味の素
PLAIN WHITE RICE	ごはん
SEAWEED	のり
FERMENTED SOYBEANS	納豆

A WAYFARER'S SERIES: THE VIEW FROM ABOVE

WORDS BY AUSTIN SAILSBURY

Austin Sailsbury tells a story about the path of discovery below, of connectedness seen from above and the creative intersection of a French master and Japanese craftsmanship.

P aris, when viewed from above, is a carefully planned, beautifully realized city, with houses, boulevards, churches and rivers each in its proper place, as if the metropolis, like a disciplined topiary, was always meant to be shaped so neatly. Seen from the Eiffel Tower, the clusters of buildings are ivory-faced, nickel-hatted and elegant. Each structure is a minor variation of its neighbor; the city is governed by a dress code, a style that identifies and defines it: the "white city" by day, the City of Light by night. From high above this well-ordered masterpiece of master planning, one can imagine Paris being created in a single act of inspired and precise craftsmanship—as if some sculptor-deity long ago decided to bless the world with the gift of a great white city.

But cities, of course, are not the result of a single act of inspiration; they are the culmination of a place's geography, history and people, perpetually taking from and adding to their own history. In this way, a city, like each of its inhabitants, is a living story.

And while Paris was "remade" by Napoleon III to be more coherent, it is still very much a great patchwork with its winding streets stitching together ancient neighborhoods, its old temples worn from both use and neglect, its shops and homes and gardens colored by the light of a thousand years of human stories. Stories of struggle and hope, family and friendship, victory and defeat. Stories of ideas and revolution, disappointment and innovation. Stories of discovery and inspiration.

I stumbled into one of these Parisian stories on a summer morning: a story about art and a far-away land and the discovery of a book of mysterious pictures. Most of all, a story about the path of discovery below and of connectedness seen from above.

—

A sudden rain shower took me, seeking shelter, into La Porte du Jardin—the kind of bookshop that Parisians find remarkably unremarkable but visitors find impossibly charming—with its hand-painted sign, its humorless owner and its clusters of books stacked about with varying degrees of care. It was the kind of wonderfully manic place where, if you were in a hurry to find something specific, you probably wouldn't find anything. But if, like me, you had wandered into the Porte du Jardin by accident, well then, every book was a treasure waiting to be discovered.

I found myself drawn to the shop's stacks of *livres d'art*. All the classics were there: Michelangelo and the Italians, the American realists and, of course, the French Impressionists. But as I browsed, thumbing through books devoted to "the masters," I came to a book and a name unknown to me: Henri Rivière.

I made out from the dust jacket that Rivière was a Frenchman living in Paris and Brittany who had worked in the early 20th century. But it was the artwork itself that quickly captured my attention: the colorful prints were very 19th century with their warm pastel scenes of ordinary people and landscapes, but they were also very...*something else*. The colors were bold and neat, the figures and trees and cliffs outlined in thick, definitive lines. There was no vagueness in Rivière's intent—he wasn't creating impressions. He was creating snapshots as they might be taken through the lens of a child's imagination: peasants laying out laundry in the sun, a wave exploding against a rock, the solemn procession of pallbearers through a village. Each of the prints was simplistic and yet somehow subtly sophisticated. I was instantly charmed by the book, by the art inside it and by the unexpected delight of a new discovery.

When the rain had passed, I stepped out into the wet street, book in hand, to wander away the rest of the day. Little did I know that my chance discovery of Rivière would lead to an exploration of what it means to be inspired by the past, what it means to innovate by bridging creative and cultural islands and how even the most seemingly simple works of art can be the result of painstaking craftsmanship.

Born in France in 1864, Rivière spent his life creating. He worked in photography, set design, publishing, painting, printmaking and in creating whimsical "shadow plays" at the Chat Noir café in the Montmartre district, but Rivière is best known for his woodcut and lithographic prints. It was these bold prints that had first caught my eye, with their charming scenes of rural and urban French life, rendered with that certain warm stylistic *something else* that I couldn't exactly identify.

That something else, as it turns out, has a direct, unmistakable heritage in the stylized genre of Japanese *ukiyo-e* woodblock prints. "Ukiyo-e" translates to "pictures of the floating world," and the art form dates back to the 17th century, though other forms of woodblock printing have existed for over a thousand years. The style is quintessentially Japanese: rich in color, highly detailed and evocative of an exotic and mysterious time and place.

And this is where the story of Japanese printmaking, the Frenchman Rivière and the Wayfarer's discovery intersect. This is the view from above.

—

When I first found the book of Rivière prints in Paris, I knew nothing of ukiyo-e. After buying the book, I didn't spend much time looking into the painstaking techniques of lithography and woodblock printing. I also knew nothing of the wave of Japonisme that had swept through western Europe at the end of the 19th century, influencing Van Gogh, Monet, Pissarro, Rivière and others. I didn't know that Rivière's use of high horizon lines, shadowless, off-center subjects and diagonal axes was borrowed from the ukiyo-e master Katsushika Hokusai. But, unquestionably, the craft of Hokusai's art matriculates through Rivière's. Inspiration begets inspiration. Beauty begets beauty. This is the legacy of great craftspeople: the best of what is made by one generation lives on as seed for future makers. Woven into the history of all made things is an intricate and mysterious legacy of discovery and inspiration. In this way, creativity is a sprawling city, the architecture of the "new" being always built with the collected stones of ancestral structures.

Where Hokusai was inspired by Mt. Fuji and provincial bridges, he applied the craft of woodblock printing to create art that would eventually travel west. Nearly 100 years later, a Frenchman would fall in love with the old master's work, modernize his techniques and infuse the Japanese aesthetic with the scenes and colors of his home country. Another 100 years after that, traveling in a foreign land, I serendipitously stumbled upon a book of colorful prints that would inspire me, challenging the way I understand landscapes and composition and the use of color.

We have no choice but to live at street level—the time and place of our individual intersection with history and circumstance. But from above, from the perspective of balconies and towers and tall tree branches, that's where we can see best—where we can catch glimpses of the boulevards that connect us with the wayfarers of the past and those that will discover *our stories* in some little bookshop on a rainy morning in the future. ○○○

Austin Sailsbury works and writes in Copenhagen, Denmark, with his wife in a farmhouse that is older than America. He is currently at work on his first novel.

RED BEAN MOCHI: DOUGH

RECIPES AND FOOD STYLING BY DIANA YEN, THE JEWELS OF NEW YORK

STYLING ASSISTANTS SUSANNA MOLLER, KALI SOLACK & PHOTOGRAPHS BY SETH SMOOT

Mochi is a treat defined by texture. And when stuffed—known in Japanese tradition as *daifuku*—these pillows of pounded rice become a confectionary vessel for whatever flavor is tucked inside. Glutinous rice is the key to mochi's distinct chew, and the flavored filling, red bean paste in this case, is the secret behind its tinge of sweetness that never cloys but always lingers. Subtle and nuanced, mochi is a lovely partner for a picnic and is a perfect companion for a cup of tea.

---

1 ½ cups (6 ounces / 170 grams)
glutinous rice flour

½ cup (3.5 ounces / 100 grams) granulated sugar

1 ⅓ cups water (8.3 ounces / 245 milliliters)

2 tablespoons (0.7 ounces / 20 grams)
black sesame seeds for finishing

Cornstarch for work surface and rolling

Red bean paste

METHOD Combine the rice flour, sugar and water in a heat-proof bowl. Stir with a spatula until mixture is completely dissolved and smooth. Loosely cover bowl in plastic wrap and microwave for two minutes, then stir well. The dough should be very sticky.

Cover the bowl once again with plastic wrap and microwave for an additional minute. Repeat the microwaving process until the dough springs back when poked with a finger. Allow to rest until cool to the touch.

Dust a clean, dry work surface with cornstarch, and rub some on your hands to keep them from sticking to the dough. With your fingertips, pinch about a tablespoon-size ball of dough and work it on the palm of your hand, flattening and stretching it into a flat, circular piece about three inches in diameter.

Take approximately 1 1/2 teaspoons of the red bean paste and roll it into a ball. Place it in the center of disc of dough and pinch it closed.

As a garnish, brush each mochi lightly with water and sprinkle with sesame seeds to finish. Serve.

Note: Glutinous rice flour is available at Asian stores. When purchasing, be sure to look for the "glutinous" label and do not substitute regular rice flour.

Makes about 12 pieces

Continued on page 119

RED BEAN MOCHI: PASTE

1 cup (6.5 ounces / 185 grams) *dry red azuki beans*	*3/4 cup (5.25 ounces / 150 grams)* *granulated sugar*
Water	*Salt*

METHOD Rinse the beans in water and place in a large pot filled with water. Bring the beans to a boil over medium-high heat, then remove from the heat and drain. Return the beans to the pot, add 3 cups (24 ounces / 710 milliliters) of water and once again bring to a boil over medium-high heat. Cover the pot and reduce the heat to low. Simmer, stirring occasionally, until the beans are tender and have absorbed most of the water, 45 to 55 minutes. Should the beans dry out during the cooking period, add more water.

Stir in the sugar and a pinch of salt. Cool completely before using.

The red bean paste may be made one week ahead of time and stored in a sealed container in the refrigerator.

Note: Azuki or adzuki beans are small dry red beans. White, black, gray and spotted varieties exist, but look for the red ones for this recipe. ○○○

Makes about 2 cups

Diana Yen, who fell in love with food while at art school, is founder of the Jewels of New York, a creative studio that combines the love of cooking with the beauty of everyday things.

ESCAPE TO KAMAKURA

Some days call for getting away from the city and back to nature.
These photos were taken in Kamakura, filled with mossy forests and a
beckoning beach, just 30 miles away from Tokyo.

PHOTO ESSAY BY CHRIS & SARAH RHOADS OF WE ARE THE RHOADS

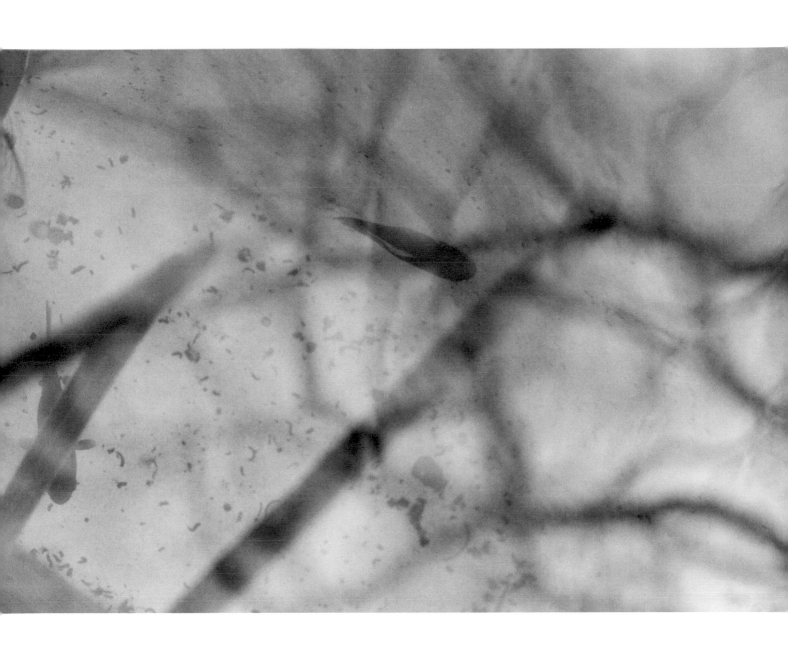

We Are the Rhoads are Chris and Sarah Rhoads, a husband-and-wife photography/directing team. They like to travel the world, working in a variety of environments.

SALT-PICKLED NAPA CABBAGE / HAKUSAI NO TSUKEMONO

RECIPE BY NANCY SINGLETON HACHISU & PHOTOGRAPH BY GENTL & HYERS

Chinese cabbage (*hakusai*) and daikon are to Japanese winter as eggplant and cucumbers are to summer. If a farming family grows nothing else, they at least grow those two vegetables during their seasons. I can still picture my father-in-law out in the field tying up his heads of Chinese cabbages to prevent the leaves from spreading out loosely. The resulting pristine, white, juicy leaves and tight cylinder shape are necessary for making cabbage pickles, since the cabbages are sliced vertically and dried in quarter wedges.

I make my pickles the old-fashioned way—in cedar buckets with drop lids and covers. Plastic tubs are certainly easier to deal with in terms of possible mold formation, but there is a deep satisfaction in making the process work the traditional way. The cedar leaches a small amount of color into the pickles, but that was always inherent in the country pickles before the post-WWII modernization of Japan.

And even if you don't achieve complete fermentation—you're not just looking for the pickles to be salty, but also pleasantly sour—you will still end up with a gently salty, citrusy, slightly spicy little vegetable condiment that anyone will willingly and happily devour!!

8 small heads Chinese or napa cabbage (1 1/3 pounds / 600 grams each), quartered vertically

1/2 cup (about 1/3 pound / 140 grams) salt

8 small garlic cloves, peeled and thinly sliced

8 small dried Japanese chili peppers or 6 árbol chilies

Zest from 4 small yuzu or Meyer lemons

METHOD Remove and discard any outer wilted leaves and dry the cabbage quarters for one day in a cool, dry place on sheets of newspaper set directly on the ground.

Line a plastic or wooden pickling tub with a large pickling-grade plastic bag. Rub each cabbage quarter with salt and pack one layer, cut sides down, on the bottom of the container. Sprinkle cabbage with some of the garlic, chilies and yuzu zest. Repeat the procedure with the remaining cabbage, salt, garlic, chilies and zest, making sure the cabbage is packed tightly.

Set the pickle tub's drop lid on top (if you don't have one, use a plate), weigh down with a rock or other heavy object (about the equivalent weight of the cabbage) and cover. Let sit outside in a cold, shady spot, out of direct sunlight, or in a cool, dry place (at about 40° to 50°F / 5° to 10°C), for a couple of weeks, checking after the first week to make sure enough brine has been exuded to cover the cabbage. If not, splash in a light 3 percent solution of salt water. If mold forms, lift it off the pickles gently and wipe any mold spots on the wooden tub with a neutral alcohol such as *shochu* or vodka.

Optimum flavor is reached after one month, but they may be eaten after one to two weeks of pickling. Pickles will keep for up to six weeks.

Note: Yuzu is an Asian citrus with uneven yellow or green skin. The aromatic fruit can be substituted with Meyer lemons.

Japanese chili peppers can be found at Asian markets and specialty stores. Árbol chilies are available in the Latin American aisle of many supermarkets, and also at specialty stores. ○○○

Serves 6

Captivated by the world of sushi, Nancy Singleton Hachisu left California for Japan in 1988, intending to learn Japanese and return to the US. Instead, she fell in love with an organic farmer. Nancy is the author of Japanese Farm Food, *a cookbook/memoir of life and food on their Japanese farm.*

SUMMER MIXTAPE

COMPILED BY BOB STANLEY & PHOTOGRAPH BY LOU MORA

*Bob Stanley, music writer and member of the London
pop group Saint Etienne, knows a thing or two about Japanese pop.
Here are 15 of his top tunes.*

T his selection is made up of Japanese female vocal pop from the mid-'60s to the recent past. The oldest song is by Emy Jackson, who was born in Japan but raised in England; "Crying in a Storm" is from 1966. There's a smattering of '90s Shibuya-Kei sounds from Pizzicato Five and Kahimi Karie, whose "David Hamilton" was written by the rakish Momus. Plus, there's a touch of fine Japanese indie by Teeny Frahoop, and UK garage-influenced "pakuri pop" from M-Flo (warning: includes some male vocal). Visit kinfolk.com/japan-mixtape to have a listen. Enjoy! ○○○

Bob Stanley writes for The Guardian *and* The Times *in England, and his book* Yeah Yeah Yeah: The Story of Modern Pop *will be published by Faber & Faber in October.*

THE EXPATS

New York's fierce electric vibe comes from all the creative energy brought in from its inhabitants. These six artisans have made it work in the city.

WORDS BY RACHEL JONES & PHOTOGRAPHS BY ADAM PATRICK JONES

NAME		OCCUPATION
Ayaka Nishi		Jewelry Designer
AGE	BORN	LIVES
34	Kagoshima	East Village
HANGS OUT		YEARS IN NYC
East Village, Lower East Side, Williamsburg		8

NAME		OCCUPATION
Makoto Suzuki		Restaurant Owner/Chef *(Bozu, Samurai Mama, Momo Sushi Shack)*
AGE	BORN	LIVES
50	Saitama	Williamsburg
HANGS OUT		YEARS IN NYC
Chelsea, Lower East Side		19

"People think 'cute' is a great compliment, but my style isn't really cute," says jewelry designer Ayaka, who felt pressure to create more feminine designs in Japan. "I want to create something I can keep for a long time." Her aesthetic relies on organic shapes and an eerie apprehension of skeletal forms—textured honeycomb-like rings and layered leather necklaces reminiscent of fish scales (one is called the Gold Ribs Spine Bracelet, named for the cuff of seven spines that protrude from the main "vertebrae" of the bracelet). Her taste for the natural world is hereditary. "It's the environment that I grew up in. My mother is an ikebana floral artist, so I was able to play with flowers and natural materials. My father was a doctor and I was very curious about anatomical images."

"Some people want to make traditional Japanese food in exactly the same way [in America], but it's impossible," says Makoto. "The ingredients are different—even the environment is different. But I can bring an experience to the customer that they can only have in Williamsburg." He moved to New York in 1994 to act on Broadway, but to get a visa, he worked at Kodama in Hell's Kitchen. For a decade, he couldn't return to Japan since his visa had expired. Finally, at age 40, he got a green card and had a wasabi-inflected epiphany. "I realized I was free. I wanted to start my own restaurant." Since then he has created a food empire spun of steaming bowls of udon and artfully combined sushi, endearing himself to critics and locals.

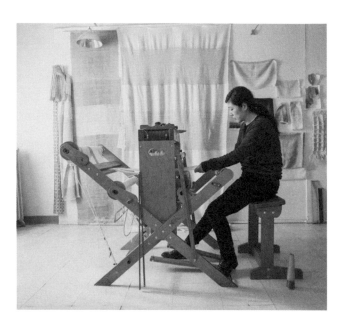

NAME		OCCUPATION
Hiroko Takeda		Textile Designer
AGE	BORN	LIVES
46	Nogoya	Brooklyn Heights
HANGS OUT		YEARS IN NYC
Cobble Hill, Carroll Gardens, Atlantic Avenue		10

NAME		OCCUPATION
Risa Nishimori		Pottery Teacher *(Togei Kyoshitsu Studio)*
AGE	BORN	LIVES
30	New York	Roosevelt Island
HANGS OUT		YEARS IN NYC
Chelsea, Lower East Side		30

"You can't do what I do in Japan. In Japan we have a very precious old traditional culture, but at present, people live in very cluttered houses," says Hiroko. "There's no market." She was trained in very basic, traditional Japanese textile techniques: ikat, stencil, tie-dye. "I remember when I got into that school, my grandmother asked, 'Do you need to go to the university to study that? That's what village people do!'" Hiroko honed her craft in London at the Royal College of Art, won a design competition and was offered a job in New York. In 2010 her employer relocated to France. "I knew at some point that I needed to leave to do my own thing," says Hiroko. She began designing and weaving her own custom textiles in Brooklyn, and she now lists Calvin Klein Home and Donna Karan New York as clients.

"It's mainly people that are born into a certain family, because they continue the tradition their family has had for generations," Risa says of those who train in ceramics, one of three culturally revered art forms in Japan (along with flower arranging and textiles). Technically not an expat, she seems comfortable in her role imparting lessons on traditional Japanese hand-building and wheel-throwing pottery techniques in the heart of Manhattan. Her parents originally came to New York from Shikoku, the smallest of Japan's four main islands, famous for its high divorce rates and bonito plates. They took pottery lessons and bought a studio in 1994. Now, 19 years later, Risa manages the studio.

NAME		OCCUPATION
Jun Aizaki		Architect *Crème Design*
AGE	BORN	LIVES
40	Saitama	Williamsburg
HANGS OUT		YEARS IN NYC
Williamsburg		20

NAME		OCCUPATION
Masamichi Udagawa		Co-founder *Antenna Design*
AGE	BORN	LIVES
48	Tokyo	Financial District
HANGS OUT		YEARS IN NYC
East Village, Lower East Side, Williamsburg		17

"I feel like I have an advantage—not because I'm Japanese, but because I'm from somewhere else," says Jun, whose firm Crème has recently worked with some choice clients, such as Danji and Red Farm, while maintaining partnerships with prestigious chefs such as *Iron Chef* winner Jose Garces. In fact, Jun has designed all seven of Garces' Philadelphia restaurants. "It's strange," says Jun. "A lot of the projects we're known for are Latin, which has nothing to do culturally with Japan, but I feel like we fit right in. We're here [in New York], but we're from somewhere else."

"I was very influenced by the city, especially by the Subway walk," says Masamichi of his adopted hometown. He designed the latest wave of NYC Subway cars and ticket vending machines for the MTA, as well as the JetBlue check-in kiosks and Bloomberg displays. "As a product designer, I always have to think about the user: Who is going to use it? How? For a long time, the user was an abstract concept. But when we started on the Subway project and the first Metro vending machine, you feel the body mass of the user. They don't go away." He has sought to marry his classic, streamlined aesthetic with a weighty attention to efficiency. "If something can be realized with less materials, less energy, less pieces, less process, less complication, it is more elegant." ○○○

Adam Patrick Jones and Rachel Jones live and work in New York. They enjoy coffee on the stoop, people-watching and telling stories. On the weekends you can find them documenting New Yorkers with an entrepreneurial spirit via their online periodical Industry of One.

SPECIAL THANKS
Paintings Katie Stratton
The Tsuji family
The Niimi family
Partnership with Kodak

Kodak
PROFESSIONAL Products

ON THE COVER
Fog Linen designer Rieko Ohashi
Photograph by Parker Fitzgerald

LOVES FOOD, WILL TRAVEL
Production coordinator and translator
Takamasa Kikuchi

IKEBANA: LEARNING TO BRANCH OUT
Photo assistant James Fitzgerald

OLD LIVES TALES
Proverbs chosen from linguanaut.com

TREE TO TEA: THE LIFE OF LEAVES
Production coordinator and translator Takamasa Kikuchi
Tea buyer Yasuhisa Iwasaki, Maruhide Iwasaki Seichaw
Tea farm/field Jiro Katahira, Houkouen
Tea blender/nose master Fumio Maeda,
from Maeda Kotaro Shoten

RECIPE: MATCHA
Styling assistants Susanna Moller & Kali Solack
Cast iron pot Korin (korin.com)

RECIPE: RED BEAN MOCHI
Styling assistants Susanna Moller & Kali Solack
Linens Sri Threads (srithreads.com)
Noguchi lamp The Noguchi Museum (noguchi.org)

—

ENDNOTES

THE LANDSCAPE OF FLAWS
Teiji Itoh, *Space and Illusion in the Japanese Garden*,
translated by Ralph Friedrich and Masajiro Shimamura
(New York: Weatherhill, 1973), 15.

Robyn Griggs, "Wabi-Sabi Time," from *Less is More:
Embracing Simplicity for a Healthy Planet, a Caring
Economy and Lasting Happiness*, editors Cecile Andrews
and Wanda Urbanska (New York: New Society
Publishers, 2009), 159.

Crispin Sartwell, *Six Names of Beauty*
(London: Routledge, 2004), 83.

WASABI HARVEST
Natsu Shimamura, "Wasabi," *The Tokyo Foundation*,
June 2, 2009 (tokyofoundation.org/en/topics/
japanese-traditional-foods/vol.-18-wasabi).

World of Wasabi, run by Michel Van Mellaerts, various
articles, accessed March 28, 2013 (wasabi.org).

FORM AND FUNCTION
Thanks to Kathryn Manzella and Ai Kanazawa of
Studio KotoKoto for speaking with *Kinfolk* about
Japanese ceramics, *yo no bi* and *mingei*
(studiokotokoto.com/about-kotokoto).

Thanks also to Rowland Ricketts for speaking
with *Kinfolk* about the indigo dyeing process
and the plants he grows and nurtures to make
indigo dye (rickettsindigo.com).

KEEPING TIME
Thanks to Martha Robinson for speaking with *Kinfolk*
about *ichi-go ichi-e* and *mono no aware* and about how
each of the two concepts is heavily influenced by, and
seen through the lens of, the other.

WABI-SABI PEACE
Robyn Griggs Lawrence, *The Wabi-Sabi House:
The Japanese Art of Imperfect Beauty* (New York:
Clarkson Potter, 2004).

Andrew Juniper, *Wabi Sabi: The Japanese Art of
Impermanence* (Tuttle Publishing, 2003)

Junichiro Tanizaki, *In Praise of Shadows*, translated
by Thomas J. Harper and Edward G. Seidensticker
(Leete's Island Books, 1977).

TREE TO TEA: THE LIFE OF LEAVES
Diana Rosen, *The Book of Green Tea*
(Storey Publishing, 1998).

Kevin Gascoyne, François Marchand, Jasmin Desharnais
and Hugo Americi, *Tea: History, Terroirs, Varieties*
(Buffalo, New York: Firefly Books, 2011).

Dawn L. Campbell, *The Tea Book* (Gretna,
Louisiana: Pelican Publishing Company, 1995).

A WAYFARER'S SERIES: THE VIEW FROM ABOVE
Valérie Sueur-Hermel, *Henri Rivière: Paysages
Bretons: Études de Vagues* (Langlaude, 2011).

Armond Fields, *Henri Rivière* (Olympic
Marketing Corp, 1983).

WWW.KINFOLK.COM

KEEP IN TOUCH